It Happened In Series

It Happened In Indiana

Remarkable Events That Shaped History

Jackie Sheckler Finch

gpp

Guilford, Connecticut

Copyright © 2011 by Morris Book Publishing, LLC

Map: Daniel Lloyd © 2011 by Morris Book Publishing, LLC

Library of Congress Cataloging-in-Publication Data is available on file.

ISBN 978-0-7627-6023-7

Printed in the United States of America

10 9 8 7 6 5 4 3 2

This book is dedicated to my family—Kelly Rose; Mike Peters; Sean Rose, Devin, Dylan, and Emma; Stefanie Rose, Will, Trey, and Arianna Scott; and Logan Peters, Miranda, and Olivia.

Thanks to Fred Foley for the memories, to his wife, Dorothy, for her friendship, and to Barb Williams Bruine for her warm hospitality.

A special remembrance to my husband, Bill Finch, whose spirit goes with me every mile and step of the way through life's journey.

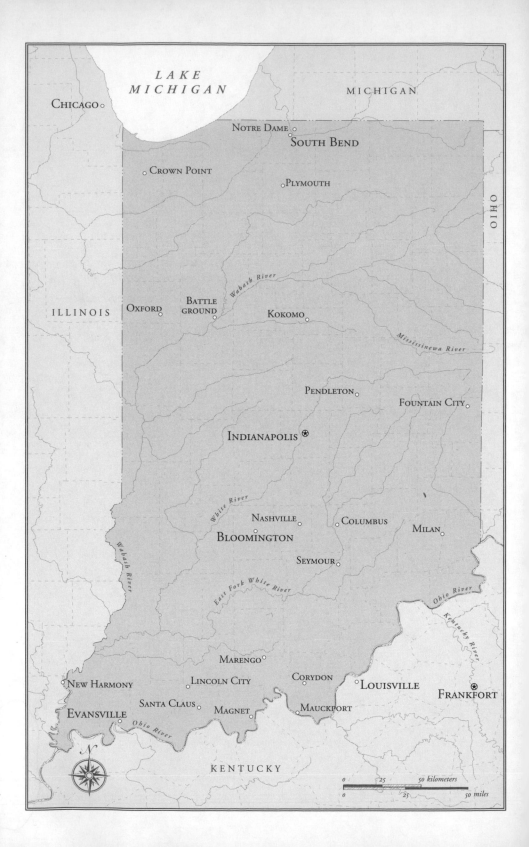

CONTENTS

CONTENTS

INTRODUCTION

When I moved to Indiana more than twenty years ago, my friends and coworkers in Massachusetts usually mentioned their two main impressions about my new home—Larry Bird and the Indy 500.

That was first and foremost what the state of Indiana brought to their minds. It is true that the great Bird (a former Boston Celtic, now the Pacers basketball president) and the world-famous auto race are a big part of what makes Indiana special. But there is so much more. I am still discovering little gems about the place I now call home.

Folks used to joke that Indiana was a "fly-over state"—that there was no reason to stop in Hoosier land. But people didn't just pass through. The heart of the Heartland, Indiana's central location, access to transportation, and economic potential meant that a wide variety of people decided to call Indiana home.

The name "Indiana" simply means "land of the Indians." When the first settlers arrived in the area, a large number of Indians were already here. The majority of Indians living in Indiana belonged to the Miami tribe, part of the Algonquin group of Indians. By the early 1800s, however, Indian tribes had almost completely disappeared from Indiana, dying from wars or European diseases or being forcibly removed to other places.

In 1679 French explorer Robert LaSalle claimed the honor as the first white man to set foot in Indiana. He and his men camped along the south bend of the St. Joseph River. The place later became the city of South Bend.

Traveling from the St. Joseph River down the Kankakee, LaSalle eventually ended up in the Mississippi River, claiming all the land around the Mississippi and its tributaries for France. In honor of French King Louis, LaSalle named the new land Louisiana. At the time, Indiana was part of that new Louisiana.

Many other Europeans, especially of French descent, followed LaSalle into the area he had claimed for France. Trading posts and forts sprang up around Indiana. The first fort, Fort Miami, was built around 1715 along the Maumee River. The city of Fort Wayne is located there now.

In 1732 a very large fort was constructed on the Wabash River and named Fort Vincennes for the French officer in command. Vincennes had an early population of three hundred people, which made it the largest French town in Indiana.

George Rogers Clark played a very important role in the history of Indiana. One of the first pioneer settlers in the state of Kentucky, Clark was concerned that the English couldn't be driven out of the Ohio Valley. Meeting with Virginia Governor Patrick Henry in 1777, Clark volunteered to lead a secret mission to attack English forts throughout the Ohio Valley.

Raising a small army of about 150 pioneer farmers, Clark headed for Vincennes, helped by French settlers in return for promising freedom of religion for them. In the winter of 1779, Clark and his growing army marched through frozen swamps and marshes to the fort at Vincennes, raising an American flag over it before heading on.

When British commander Henry Hamilton heard about Clark's victories, he decided to attack the Americans at Vincennes. Hamilton took the fort without firing a shot. Knowing that he didn't have the men to fight Hamilton in a regular military battle, Clark decided to make a surprise attack. In February of 1779, Clark and about 180 men began a slow, torturous march toward Vincennes. In the depths of winter, the land was frozen and much of it was flooded. Clark's men had to sleep in the shallowest pools of water they could find.

About twenty miles outside Vincennes, the water became waist high. Unable to hunt for food or to build a fire to cook it, the men trudged on, becoming weaker by the hour. Before long, the freezing water was chin high. To motivate his men, Clark plunged ahead, reportedly singing "Yankee Doodle." At last, the ragtag frozen group was two miles from Vincennes. The English inside the fort began firing on Clark and his men. But Clark's men were excellent riflemen and hunters and began to pick off the English soldiers.

Seeing his losses, Henry Hamilton surrendered to Clark. The capture of Fort Sackville at Vincennes gave the Americans control of the Ohio Valley. When the American Revolution ended in 1783, the United States gained all the land west of the Appalachian Mountains. Indiana became the nineteenth state in the Union on December 11, 1816.

Indiana is blessed with historians, historical societies, museums, and attractions that preserve the state's interesting history. Even the smallest towns seem to have groups of people and cubbyhole museums carefully collecting local stories. The twenty-five tales in this book are only a tiny fraction of the fascinating saga of Indiana.

I would especially like to thank the state historians, tourism officials, and other folks who helped me research this book. Gratitude to my Globe Pequot editor, Meredith Rufino, for believing that Indiana is filled with wonderful stories, and to my project editor, Greg Hyman, for his keen attention to detail.

We Hoosiers are friendly people, and we like to share our history and home with others. So many other stories still wait to be told. It's an honor that you have chosen this book as your companion in discovering more about Indiana. I sincerely hope it helps steer your steps into making your Hoosier historical experience a rewarding and memorable one.

CAVE SAVES SQUIRE BOONE'S LIFE

1790

Indians were hot on his heels when Squire Boone remembered a cave he and his older brother had discovered years earlier. Grabbing a stout hanging vine, Boone swung into the cave near present-day Mauckport, Indiana. Covering the entrance with branches, Boone prayed earnestly that he would not be found.

He wasn't.

Indians stomped around above the cave but evidently did not know it was there or that Boone was hidden right below their feet. Beginning that day in 1790, Boone believed the cave was Holy Ground. And he vowed to bring his family there someday. Boone also chose the small cave for his final resting place. Through a series of lucky events and perseverance, that is where the famed frontiersman is buried today

It's a weird feeling to come upon the simple walnut coffin and tombstone in the cave that now bears Squire Boone's name. The story of how Boone's remains came to be found there might be even stranger.

It all started several centuries ago. Squire Boone Sr. came to Pennsylvania from England. He and his wife, Sarah, became the parents of eleven children. The sixth child, born in 1734, was Daniel Boone—one of America's most famous pioneer adventurers. Ten years later, Squire Boone Jr. was born. Though a decade apart in age, the two brothers were almost inseparable.

Of the first eight white men who dared to enter "the dark and bloody ground," as Kentucky was known in the early 1770s, only two returned alive—Daniel and Squire Boone. Squire helped clear the Wilderness Road and in his later years was honored by Congress for his service during the Revolutionary War.

Squire fought in many hand-to-hand battles, including the Battle of Fort Boonesboro. He was wounded eleven times, taking him to death's door on several occasions. A skilled gunsmith, Squire crafted Daniel's famous "Tick Licker" rifle as a gift. That's one reason, it is said, that Daniel was such a great shot. The gun Squire had made him was built so carefully that the aim was true and helped Daniel fire more accurately.

In 1787 the brothers were exploring an area near what is now southern Indiana. Climbing a hillside, they saw a spring gushing torrents of water. Searching for the water source, the two discovered a cave entrance.

Crawling in, the Boones gazed in the flickering glow of their torches at a subterranean wonderland. Veteran cave explorers, they were nonetheless enthralled.

This cave would one day save Squire Boone's life.

After his 1790 close encounter with the Indians, Squire would often return to the cave to pray, meditate, and carve designs and verses of gratitude.

In 1804 Squire moved his wife, daughter, and four sons to the area, where they built a village and a gristmill. Squire spent the last eleven years of his life here—the longest he ever stayed in one place.

As his death neared—Squire suffered from dropsy, otherwise known as heart failure—he began constructing his own coffin from walnut trees growing near the cave.

On his deathbed, he asked his sons to bury him in the cave where the Lord had spared his life. On August 15, 1815, Squire's four sons fulfilled their father's final request. Squire was buried in his beloved cave, with a boulder sealing the entrance.

More than 150 years passed. The walnut coffin rotted. Squire's bones rested on the cave's floor and were gradually covered by years of silt. Squire had become famous by the time of his death, and people would steal pieces of his coffin as relics. But Squire's remains were still in the cave, hidden by the sands of time.

In 1973, the large cave behind the waterfall was named Squire Boone Caverns and opened to the public. Modern conveniences such as concrete walkways, handrails, and indirect lighting were installed. The project was immense and slow moving since everything had to be carried into the cave.

Thousands of visitors came to visit the cave. Like the Boones, they were thrilled by the roaring underground streams and waterfalls, the dazzling cave formations, and the massive pillars of stone.

The first year the cave was open, a visitor mentioned to the guides that he had visited the burial cave as a child. He recalled seeing the coffin and the cave carvings.

Two of the guides, brothers Rick and Allen Conway, decided to find the carvings by digging out the silt and debris that had filled up the burial section of the cave. Instead, in the summer of 1974, they found Squire himself.

First, the brothers uncovered small bones, then larger ones. And finally a skull.

Experts determined the bones, marked with old injuries—such as a tomahawk hole in the skull and a shorter right arm from a break that never mended correctly—did indeed belong to Squire Boone.

A new walnut coffin was created, and a Boone family descendant knitted a shroud for the bones. Squire Boone's remains were placed in the coffin, the lid was sealed with wax, and the coffin was carried deep into Squire Boone Caverns.

It now rests in front of several long benches where tour visitors like to stop to listen to Squire's story and pay their respects. Although most folks have heard of Daniel Boone, his brother's name is not as well known. But Squire Boone's life was equally exciting as his brother's, as a visit to Squire Boone Caverns can reveal.

Along with the caverns, an operating gristmill has been rebuilt on the original foundation used by Squire Boone. The eighteen-foot wheel is powered by waters flowing by the caverns. Inside the mill are the foundation stones, on which Squire carved the inscription:

My God my life hath much befriended, I'll praise Him til my days are ended.

BATTLE OF TIPPECANOE

1811

On a bitterly cold rainy night, Indian warriors slowly and silently crawled on their stomachs toward the campsite. Soldiers were asleep, but an alert sentry saw the Indians in their black war paint and fired a warning shot before he was killed.

For the next two hours, the bloody fighting raged. The Indians' orders were to kill Commander William Henry Harrison and his senior officers. It would be an easy task, the warriors believed, because they were protected by their mighty leader—the Prophet.

After all, hadn't the Prophet told his followers that he had the power to cheat death both in life and on the battlefield? He would make the white man's bullets as harmless as rain. He would magnify the strength of the warriors into invincible supermen.

All this the Prophet promised. Urging his followers on, the Prophet stood on a nearby hill, a safe distance from the fighting. His battle cries spurred them on, but nothing could protect the out-numbered and out-weaponed Indians. Dashing point-blank into the enemy guns, the Indians stood little chance.

Fighting alongside his men, Harrison was the victor. Years later, Harrison bragged "the Indians had never sustained so severe a defeat since their acquaintance with the white people."

How did it come to this? What brought about the slaughter on November 7, 1811, in the town now known as Battle Ground, Indiana?

It might have begun when the Shawnee baby known as Tecumseh was born March 9, 1768, in the village of Piqua, Ohio. The night of his birth, a fiery meteor streaked across the sky, signaling that this child was destined for greatness. According to tradition, the newborn was named Tecumseh, "Panther Passing Across," because of the brilliant meteor that traveled across the sky.

Even as a child, Tecumseh was a leader. Skilled with weapons as well as words, Tecumseh was an intelligent young man respected by those far older. His younger brother, Lalawethika, or "The Noisemaker," however, was just the opposite. Born in 1775, Lalawethika was clumsy, ill-tempered, boastful, and unpleasant to be around. The loss of his right eye made Lalawethika even more difficult.

Though stories about the eye loss are conflicting, one says that it happened when Lalawethika was about eleven and out with some other boys learning to hunt. Although the other boys ducked when an errant arrow came their way, Lalawethika didn't. Another story says that Lalawethika himself put out his eye by carelessly trying to kill a turkey when he was drunk, turning the bow backward so the arrow flew right into his eye.

Lalawethika was soon considered useless while his older brother was quickly becoming a rising star. Increasingly lazy, Lalawethika developed a taste for the white man's whiskey and became a burden to his family and tribe. Then one day, Lalawethika fell into a drunken stupor. When he couldn't be roused, many thought the drunkard was dead. Instead, Lalawethika roused and proclaimed that he had been gifted with a vision—that Indians should forsake the white man's way and return to the proud heritage of their ancestors.

That vision fit perfectly with Tecumseh's goals. With his new name of Tenskwatawa, meaning "Open Door" because he would be the open door through which the Great Spirit spoke, Tecumseh's brother suddenly became a man of power and respect—the Prophet. Although Tecumseh remained wary of his younger brother, the two worked together to unite Indian tribes, regain tribal land, and renounce former treaties that had cost them their homes.

As their base, the two brothers chose to build a new settlement on the high ground along the Tippecanoe River, near what is today Lafayette, Indiana. Called Tippecanoe by some and Prophetstown by others, the village had many cabins, plus a large lodge for visitors, a medicine lodge for the Prophet, and a huge council house.

At the same time that Tecumseh was trying to unite his people, William Henry Harrison was working to make Indiana a state. Appointed governor of the territory, Harrison knew that President Thomas Jefferson wanted land for Americans, and Harrison's goal was to convince the Indian nations to turn over about three million acres of land.

Using trinkets and presents, Harrison persuaded Indian chiefs to agree to new treaties and relinquish their land. But Harrison knew that Tecumseh and the Prophet stood in the way of his ultimate quest. Hoping to discredit the Prophet, Harrison asked him for a sign, proof that he had been sent by God. Maybe, Harrison suggested, the great Prophet could make the sun stand still.

Harrison's trap backfired, however. His words set the stage to have the Prophet be recognized as even more of a holy man. Replying to Harrison's letter in 1806, the Prophet said that all doubters should assemble on the morning of April 16 to watch him make the sun stand still.

How incredible, the Prophet's enemies thought. This folly would surely be his downfall. No man could stop the path of the sun. But shortly before noon on April 16, 1806, an eclipse of the sun took place—just after the Prophet had pointed to the heavens.

The astonished crowd was terrified. It was said that chickens roosted for the night and nocturnal animals crawled forth from their hiding places. For almost seven minutes, it was pitch black. Then the Prophet's voice boomed out, asking the Great Spirit to remove his hand from the face of the sun and let the earth be bright again. Sure enough, the eclipse ended. News of the Prophet's miracle soon spread, and Harrison knew he was in more trouble than ever.

How did the Prophet do such an astounding deed? Astronomers knew that the moon would pass directly between the sun and the Earth on that day, that the eclipse would block out the sun's rays and turn day into night. Some say that the Prophet heard about the eclipse. Others think that Tecumseh did and shared his knowledge with his brother. Whatever the reason, the feat elevated the Prophet even more in the eyes of the Indians.

Early in August 1811, Tecumseh set off with some of his warriors on a six-month journey to recruit more tribes to his alliance. Before leaving, he gave strict orders to his brother that the Prophet and their people in Prophetstown should do nothing to anger Harrison. The time was not right for a confrontation with Harrison, and Tecumseh made the Prophet promise that he would do nothing that could be construed as a threat to the white man.

At the same time, President Madison was warning Harrison not to force the hand of the Indians. Of course, the Prophet didn't keep his promise. And neither did Harrison.

Finding out that Tecumseh had headed south, Harrison made his move. With more than a thousand soldiers, Harrison marched toward Prophetstown and built a stockade not far from the Indian town. Then he headed into Prophetstown with the goal of wiping out the Indian capital and getting rid of the Prophet to stop Tecumseh's goal of a united Indian nation.

Hearing that Harrison and his troops were on their way, the Prophet sent out a white flag of truce, asking Harrison to meet with him the next day to seek a peaceful agreement. Accepting the truce, Harrison set up camp.

However, the Prophet broke his word to his brother and to Harrison. In the dead of night, the Prophet dispatched his warriors to kill the white men. No harm would come to the Indians, the Prophet promised his fighters. It was a slaughter.

When the Indians finally figured out that the Prophet had no powers and that the dead were piling up, the remaining warriors took off. So did the Prophet. Back in Prophetstown, the angry tribesmen threatened to kill the Prophet. He, in turn, said he would make stronger medicine to protect them if they would just regroup and fight the soldiers again. Instead, the remaining Indians left Prophetstown in disgust.

When no new assault was carried out, Harrison marched his troops to Prophetstown and burned the recently deserted place to the ground. Bragging that the Battle of Tippecanoe was a major triumph for the United States, Harrison was now a national hero, proudly nicknamed "Tippecanoe." He would ride that reputation straight to the White House with his vice presidential running mate John Tyler, using the slogan "Tippecanoe and Tyler Too."

When Tecumseh returned home and saw Prophetstown and all his work in ashes, he was furious, stripping the Prophet of any leadership powers. Tecumseh fought on and tried to unite his people before being killed at the Battle of the Thames on October 5, 1813. Tecumseh's body was never found, but legend says it was carried off by his warriors and buried in a secret place. The Prophet died in 1836 at a reservation in Kansas City, virtually a forgotten man.

Harrison, of course, went on to become the ninth President of the United States. But some say the Indian brothers exacted their revenge. On a cold wet November 4, 1841, when the sixty-seven-year-old Harrison took the oath of office, he wore neither hat nor overcoat and delivered the longest inaugural address in American history. At 8,444 words, it took nearly two hours to read. Harrison caught pneumonia and died on his thirty-second day in office—the shortest tenure in United States presidential history.

NEW HARMONY SETTLED AS
A UTOPIAN COMMUNITY

1814

It might seem a strange place to create Utopia. But two different leaders chose this southwestern Indiana spot for what they thought would be the ideal life. Although neither community lasted, each left an indelible mark on New Harmony and on the world.

Of course, George Rapp probably didn't realize what an important step he was taking when he bought thirty thousand acres of land along the Wabash River in 1814. "Father" Rapp led a group of eight hundred Harmonists to the United States from Germany to escape religious persecution. They came to Indiana from Pennsylvania. Within a year, the Harmonists had created a planned community in the wilderness of the Indiana territory. From 1814 to 1824, the Harmonists perfected a cosmopolitan and industrious community while awaiting the millennium.

The Harmonists expected the return of Christ every day, so they felt each day could be their last. The Harmonists also believed in celibacy, which is why the society died out near the end of the 1800s. Since the Harmonists expected each day to be their last, they didn't worry about New Harmony surviving or about a future. Above all, Rapp preached love, and he carved a golden rose in the wood over the door of the church as the symbol of the Harmonie community.

An industrious people, the Harmonists established many successful industries including the making of fine silks and distilling of whiskey. They worked hard, wasted nothing, and within five years Harmonie was said to be the most prosperous town in Indiana. With its manicured gardens and neat, tree-lined street, Harmonie was known for its beauty. The land was planted with a 150-acre vineyard and a 35-acre orchard of choice apple and pear trees. While other settlers built only with logs, the Harmonists constructed with bricks as well as carefully shaped logs. Many of their buildings are still standing today. By 1824, Harmonie boasted more than 180 structures, including more than 126 family dwelling houses. Harmonie was largely self-sufficient and had a steam engine, two large granaries, a cocoonery, silk factory, oil mill, sawmill, brickyard, brewery, wool and cotton factories, a threshing machine, and a five-acre vegetable garden. A portable greenhouse was constructed for raising oranges and lemons. Over twenty products— including boots, wagons, hats, cloth, produce, harnesses, and whiskey—were being marketed as far away as Pittsburgh and New Orleans.

However, the Harmonists were not well liked by their neighbors. They spoke German, kept to themselves, and were usually more successful than other farmers, builders, and traders. So in 1825, Rapp decided to return his group to Pennsylvania. Difficulties in shipping goods, problems with malaria, and a hope to rekindle the spirit of his followers may have contributed to the decision.

Rapp put the whole town along with its 30,000 acres of land up for sale. Rapp sold the entire town to a wealthy Welsh-born social reformer, Robert Owen, who bought it for $150,000, far less than the value of the property alone.

Like Rapp, Owen also had a dream—to create a model community where educational and social equality would prosper. But after that common dream, the two men were greatly different. Owen was an atheist and felt that the church, as well as marriage and private property ownership, were detriments to society. Owen believed that environment contributed to character and a society could be perfect with an ideal environment. For his utopia, Owen looked to human reason and science rather than toward heaven. Along with his partner, geologist and educator William Maclure, Owen renamed the town New Harmony and began one of the most remarkable social experiments in America.

Scholars, scientists, and educators from Europe and America were drawn to New Harmony to establish this enlightened communal living settlement. It became an intellectual haven. In fact, several outstanding people of the day arrived in a boat called *The Philanthropist*, often referred to as "The Boatload of Knowledge."

Owen believed that early education was essential for happiness and success—his philosophy of "Universal Happiness through Universal Education." He organized the first kindergarten in America in New Harmony. True community labor, he believed, would be a pleasure, and no one would have to work more than a few hours a day in this ideal world.

New Harmony attracted some remarkably talented people: the nation's most distinguished zoologist Thomas Say, biologist and artist Charles Lesueur, educator Joseph Neef, and feminist and socialist Frances Wright.

Sadly, harmony did not reign in the utopia. Great thinkers are not necessarily great doers. Buildings fell into disrepair, weeds sprouted in previously immaculate gardens and lawns, hogs got loose and devoured vegetable gardens, and little work was done. Owen's dream failed and was dissolved in 1827. Owen returned to Scotland, but his daughter and four of his sons remained in New Harmony, along with Maclure and other "Owenites."

Owen's community had an immense impact on the nation's art and architecture, public education system, women's suffrage movement, industrial development in the Midwest, and much more.

It boasted one of the country's first infant schools and kindergartens, as well as one of the first trade schools, a free public library, an early women's club, a free public school system, a civic drama club, and the departing point for early federal geological surveys led by David Dale Owen.

When the Civil War erupted, the enlightened community seemed forgotten. But descendants of the Owenites wanted to preserve New Harmony's heritage. In the early 1940s, a descendant of Robert Owen brought his bride to his ancestral home. Jane Blaffer Owen fell in love with New Harmony and determined to help save it and its special spirit.

The Roofless Church was designed as an interdenominational spiritual retreat. It was Jane Blaffer Owen's belief that "only one roof, the sky, could embrace all worshipping humanity."

To share New Harmony with visitors, she created the New Harmony Inn and the Red Geranium Restaurant, as well as the Red Geranium Bookstore. The restaurant is well known for its hearty fare and lemon pie.

The town also has plenty of shops brimming with antiques, books, and handmade gifts. Galleries and garden shops continue the nineteenth-century tradition. Once called "The Athens of the West," New Harmony is still a favorite place to rejuvenate the spirit.

The best place to start a visit of New Harmony is at The Atheneum Visitors Center. It's easy to pick out because The Atheneum doesn't look like any of the other historic wooden structures. A gleaming white structure, The Atheneum was built in 1979 as a striking contrast to most of the village. The ultra-modern building, rising from a meadow near the riverbank, has garnered awards for its architectural design.

In addition to the Roofless Church, two interesting spots are the Harmonist Cemetery and the Cathedral Labyrinth and Sacred Garden. Site of about 230 burials, the cemetery has no markers. That's in keeping with their belief in equality. They are equal in death as well as in life.

The Cathedral Labyrinth and Sacred Garden is patterned after one dating back to the twelfth century, The Cathedral of Notre Dame's labyrinth in Chartres, France. Christians have used the labyrinth in symbolic pilgrimages, and variations of the theme are documented throughout history. For instance, European coastal fishermen would walk a labyrinth ceremoniously before heading out to sea. During the Harmonist era here, the small temple and garden maze were considered a place to relax after a long workday. Unlike a maze, a labyrinth has no dead ends or wrong turns. It is not a puzzle. It is meant to calm the spirit—a fitting symbol for New Harmony.

ABRAHAM LINCOLN MOVES TO INDIANA

1816

The young boy knelt before a grave, telling his baby brother good-bye. It was December 1816, and the family was leaving Knob Creek, Kentucky, for the Indiana frontier.

But first, seven-year-old Abraham Lincoln wanted to visit his brother Thomas's final resting spot. The baby had lived only long enough to receive his father's name.

Although it was early winter, Thomas and Nancy Hanks Lincoln were leaving their Kentucky home. Tired of trouble over property rights, the Lincolns decided life would be better in Indiana, where people could buy land directly from the government. Besides, Thomas Lincoln did not believe in slavery, and Indiana had no slavery.

The family had no way of knowing that their son would grow up to become the sixteenth President of the United States. Living in Indiana from a youngster of seven to a young man of twenty-one, Abraham Lincoln later said that he gained many of his values and skills as a Hoosier. The oft-quoted man said, "Here I grew up," when recalling his life in the Indiana wilderness from 1816 to 1830.

After arriving at his 160-acre claim near the Little Pigeon Creek in what is now Spencer County, Thomas quickly set about building a cabin and carving a new life from the "wild region," as Abraham once described the largely unsettled Indiana woodlands. When the Lincoln family arrived in this area, they had to hack out a trail by hand. Indiana was a wilderness then, a forest of giant oaks, maples, and hickories where open views of even two hundred yards were rare.

Though Abe was only seven years old, he later remembered the trip to Little Pigeon Creek as one of the hardest experiences of his life. Lincoln himself described it in a poem he wrote many years after leaving the state:

"When first my father settled here,
'Twas the frontier line.
The panther's scream filled the night with fear,
And bears preyed on the swine."

Abe worked with his father—splitting rails, plowing and planting, building a cabin, and drawing water from a spring. The log cabin was only eighteen feet square with a packed dirt floor and a stone fireplace used for both cooking and heating. Abe described the place as "the very spot where grew the bread that formed my bones."

Although he was still a child, Abe was large for his age and had enough strength to swing an ax. For as long as he lived in Indiana, he was seldom without his ax. He later called it "that most useful instrument."

In the fall of 1818, tragedy struck the family. Nancy Hanks Lincoln went to tend some neighbors who were ill. As "milk sickness" struck the Little Pigeon Creek settlement, Abraham's mother herself became a victim. Although they didn't know it back then, milk sickness was caused by the white snakeroot plant. The illness was most common in dry years when cows wandered from poor pastures into the woods in search of food. The illness developed when a person ate the butter or drank the milk of an animal that had eaten the plant. Similar to arsenic, the white snakeroot plant has pretty white flowers in late summer, but it is toxic.

Recovery was slow and might never be complete. But more often an attack was fatal. So it was for Nancy Hanks Lincoln. On October 5, 1818, she died. Thomas and Abraham hammered together a rough wooden coffin, and the family buried wife and mother on a wooded knoll south of the cabin. Abraham was only nine; his sister Sarah was eleven.

The death was a hard blow to the family. Dennis Hanks, an eighteen-year-old cousin whose parents also had died from milk sickness, lived with them now. In November 1819, Thomas journeyed back to Kentucky in search of a new wife. He found her in Sarah Bush Johnston, a widow with three children.

On December 2, 1819, they were married in Elizabethtown, Kentucky. Thomas seemed to have chosen well, for the cheerful and orderly Sarah proved to be a kind stepmother who reared Abraham and his sister as her own, encouraging the children to study. Sarah brought many books and household furnishings with her to Indiana. Thomas never fully understood Abe's desire to read and learn, but Sarah supported her stepson's ambitions.

Abe attended the Little Pigeon River Primitive Baptist Church and received little formal education. As he later recalled, his education was gotten "by littles" and the total "did not amount to one year." At the age of eleven, Abe acquired and read Parson Weems's *Life of Washington,* followed by Benjamin Franklin's *Autobiography, Robinson Crusoe,* and *The Arabian Nights.* Abe could often be seen toting a book as well as an ax and would prop himself up under a tree or by the light of the fireplace to read whenever he could.

Young Abe loved to wrestle and was recognized as one of the area's best tusslers. His great physical strength earned him the nickname "Young Hercules of Pigeon Creek," and he could hoist more weight and drive an ax deeper than anyone around. By the time he was nineteen, he had reached his full height of six feet, four inches.

In late 1828, James Gentry, the richest man in the community, hired Abe to accompany his son Allen to New Orleans in a flatboat loaded with produce. Down the Ohio they floated and into the Mississippi. At New Orleans they sold their cargo and flatboat and rode a steamboat back home. For his three months' work, Abe earned $24.

But, more importantly, the trip gave him his first view of the world beyond his own community. It showed him the evil face of slavery. While in New Orleans, Abraham witnessed a slave auction on the docks. It was an experience that greatly disturbed him—and one that he never forgot.

That same year, Abe's sister died in childbirth at age twenty. Her child, a boy, was stillborn. Sarah Lincoln Grigsby was buried with her baby in the churchyard behind the Little Pigeon Creek Baptist Church. Her husband, Aaron Grigsby, who outlived her by only three years, was later buried beside her. Their graves are now located within the boundary of Lincoln State Park.

The two most important women in young Abe's life were now gone. The following year, the Lincolns decided to quit Indiana for the fertile prairies of Illinois. In fourteen years, Thomas Lincoln had wrung only a modest living from his land. The family also feared a new outbreak of the terrible scourge of milk sickness.

Again, Abraham Lincoln bid farewell at another grave—that of his mother. Abraham Lincoln, product of the Kentucky hills and Indiana forests, was on his way to his place in history.

LEVI COFFIN AND THE
UNDERGROUND RAILROAD

1820s–1840s

Clutching her baby, the escaped slave arrived at the home seeking a place to hide and food to eat. Levi Coffin didn't turn her away. He and his wife, Catharine, had sheltered hundreds of runaway slaves on the Underground Railroad. The woman and child stayed several days at the Coffin home in Newport, Indiana.

It wasn't until years later that Coffin discovered the slave's identity and her important place in the struggle to abolish slavery. The woman he had helped was the real Eliza Harris of *Uncle Tom's Cabin* fame. She was the slave who crossed the Ohio River on the drifting ice with her child in her arms. Eliza's story was graphically told by author Harriet Beecher Stowe in the book that was said to have helped start the Civil War.

"The cruelties of slavery depicted in that remarkable work are not overdrawn," Coffin later said. "The stories are founded on facts that really occurred."

Only the names of characters in the book were changed to protect real people, such as those who ran the Underground Railroad.

In *Uncle Tom's Cabin,* Coffin and his wife were named Simeon and Rachel Halliday, a Quaker couple who helped Eliza in her escape.

Years later, in 1854, Coffin and his wife were visiting Chatham, Canada. At the close of a meeting at one of the black churches, a woman came up, grasped his wife's hand, and exclaimed, "God bless you!"

Although the Coffins didn't recognize the woman, she knew them and thanked them for their kindness in sheltering her and her baby for several days during her escape. That woman was Eliza Harris. "We visited her at her house while at Chatham and found her comfortable and contented," Coffin said.

Other former fugitives came up and blessed the Coffins for their long-ago assistance. "Such circumstances occurred in nearly every neighborhood we visited in Canada," Coffin recalled in the book *Fleeing For Freedom.*

"Hundreds who had been sheltered under our roof and fed at our table, when fleeing from the land of whips and chains, introduced themselves to us and referred to the time, often fifteen or twenty years before, when we had aided them," he said.

Born in 1798 in New Garden, North Carolina, Levi Coffin was brought up to be a farmer and a Quaker like his father. As a child, Coffin saw white owners abusing their black slaves. He dates his own personal conversion to abolitionism to an incident that occurred when he was only seven years old. Chopping wood with his father, Coffin saw a group of slaves handcuffed and chained together being herded along the roadside for sale to another plantation.

In answer to his son's question about why they were chained, the elder Coffin said the men were bound so that they could not escape and return to their wives and children. It was inconceivable to the young boy that his own father could ever be taken away from him like that.

That moment, Coffin later said, was the awakening of a deep sympathy in him for the oppressed and a hatred of oppression and injustice of any kind. By the time he was fifteen, Coffin and his cousin Vestal Coffin had frequently helped slaves on their way north. Runaways knew that they could find refuge in the fields surrounding the Coffin farm. Going about his chores, young Coffin would share his own food with the hiding slaves and warn them when they should stay hidden and when it was safe to venture on.

It was dangerous to be a runaway slave or a person helping those seeking freedom. In 1793, the First Fugitive Slave Act passed, authorizing any free state in the Union or territories northwest or south of the Ohio River to return any person who had fled slavery.

As North Carolina became more and more oppressive to those who opposed slavery, Coffin moved to Indiana in 1822. Now twenty-four years old, Coffin knew that the free state of Indiana would allow him and other Quakers to live their principles with fewer restrictions.

On October 28, 1824, Levi Coffin and his childhood friend, Catharine White, were married. The Coffins set up housekeeping in Newport, Indiana (now Fountain City), in 1826. The Coffins offered their home as a shelter, and it soon became well known to escaping slaves. It is estimated that the Coffins helped over 2,000 fugitives during their twenty years in Newport and another 1,100 while at Cincinnati.

Running a general store, the Coffins built a new dwelling in 1839 as a home for themselves and their six children. But it was also intended as a safe house on the Underground Railroad. A room at the rear of the house was built with five different doorways so if a bounty hunter or slave owner knocked at the front door, there were still plenty of escape exits for any freedom seekers hiding in the home. One of the home's bedrooms also had an entrance to a small garret where slaves could hide.

In the case of Eliza Harris, Coffin later told her story in the book *Reminiscences of Levi Coffin.* A slave in Kentucky, Eliza lived a few miles back from the Ohio River, below Ripley, Ohio. Her master and mistress were kind to her and she had a comfortable home until her master ran into financial problems. To raise money, her master decided to sell Eliza and separate her from her child.

"She had buried two children and was doubly attached to the one she had left," Coffin wrote. "When she found out that it was to be taken from her, she was filled with grief and dismay and resolved to make her escape that night if possible."

When darkness fell and the family was asleep, Eliza slipped off with her child in her arms and walked straight to the Ohio River. "She knew that it was frozen over at that season of the year, and hoped to cross without difficulty on the ice, but when she reached its banks at daylight, she found that the ice had broken up and was slowly drifting in large cakes," Coffin said.

Venturing to a nearby house, Eliza was welcomed to remain the day. Her plans were to find a way to cross the river that night. During the day, however, the ice became even more broken and dangerous to cross. When pursuers came near the house where she was hiding, Eliza vowed to cross the river to freedom or die trying.

With her pursuers right behind her, Eliza ran to the river and jumped on a large cake of ice, then sprang from that to another and another. "Sometimes the cake she was on would sink beneath her weight, then she would slide her child on to the next cake, pull herself with her hands and so continue her hazardous journey," Coffin wrote.

Frozen and numb from the icy water, Eliza did make it to the other shore. But she was too exhausted and breathless to pull her child and herself up on the bank. "A man who had been standing on the bank watching her progress with amazement and expecting any moment to see her go down assisted her up the bank," Coffin wrote.

Eliza was taken to the nearby home of the Reverend John Rankin, whose Ripley dwelling was on the Underground Railroad. There Eliza and her child were warmed, but it was deemed too dangerous for her to stay there. Her pursuers might be right behind her. For her safety, Eliza was sent to Newport, Indiana, and the home of Levi and Catharine Coffin.

On April 22, 1847, the Coffins moved to Cincinnati, Ohio, to help start a Free Store, a shop that would carry only merchandise supplied by free labor, none from slave work. The Coffins planned to stay only five years in Cincinnati. They stayed thirty years and continued their efforts in the Underground Railroad. Levi Coffin died at his Cincinnati home on September 16, 1877. He was seventy-nine years old.

Several black men served as pallbearers at his funeral. It is common that a Quaker grave be unmarked or have no standing headstone to honor the deceased. However, in 1902, a six-foot-tall monument was unveiled by the black people of Cincinnati at the Cumminsville cemetery. Catharine Coffin died in 1881 and was buried next to her husband. Inscribed on the stone are the words: NOBLE BENEFACTORS. AIDING THOUSANDS TO GAIN FREEDOM, A TRIBUTE FROM THE COLORED PEOPLE OF CINCINNATI, OHIO.

The Levi Coffin House in Fountain City, Indiana, is now a National Historic Landmark and is open to the public. Bought by the state of Indiana in 1967, the house has been well preserved and restored to the period when Levi and Catharine Coffin lived there and welcomed so many escaping slaves to their home.

STATE CAPITAL MOVES TO INDIANAPOLIS

1824

In late 1824, a wagon train left southern Indiana bound for the new state capital in a fledgling city known as Indianapolis. For eight years, Corydon had been the capital of Indiana and the move—only 125 miles away—took an arduous fourteen days. The goal was to have the new capital settled so the legislature could meet there in January of 1825.

"I could not ride in the wagon as it was covered and made me sick," Mary Anderson Naylor recalled. "I walked the eleven miles of our first day's journey."

Mary was just a young girl when her family moved. Her sister Lydia was married to a lawyer named Samuel Merrill, who had been appointed state treasurer. The family lived in the state capital of Corydon at the time, so when the capital moved to Indianapolis, state officials had to move, too. They also had to transport all the records, books, treasury, and other items that the new government had accumulated for state business.

"The road was laid with rails or logs for miles, then covered with water that seemed bottomless," Mary wrote in an historical account. "When the horse and wagon would go down, it seemed they might have reached China."

Roads were so bad, she recalled, that one day the group traveled only two and a half miles. "The water lay in the road too deep to venture in, and trees had to be felled to make a road around."

So why did folks decide that the capital no longer should be in Corydon? That's a fairly easy answer. The hard question is why it was located in Corydon in the first place.

Turn back the clock more than two hundred years ago. Corydon was laid out in 1808 by Henry Heth on land bought from William Henry Harrison—the man who went on to win the Battle of Tippecanoe in 1811 and became president of the United States in 1841. Back in 1808, Harrison was governor of the Indiana Territory. He had named the settlement Corydon for the young shepherd boy who died in Harrison's favorite hymn, "The Pastoral Elegy," which was in the popular songbook *Old Missouri Harmony*.

It was in Corydon that Indiana delegates met to draft the first state constitution on June 10, 1816. Other towns had initially been under consideration for the new capital, and no one seems to know why Corydon was picked since it was located in the southern part of the state and was difficult to reach. Only forty feet square, the little two-story limestone courthouse that had recently been built was getting quite warm and crowded, so the forty-three representatives moved their work outside to the shade of a huge elm tree. Standing about two hundred yards northwest of the courthouse near Big Indian Creek, the sheltering tree became known as "Constitution Elm." Legend says that the men kept their jugs of fortifying drink cooling in the creek.

The group drafting the state document was composed of twenty-three lawyers, five ministers, veterans of the Battle of Tippecanoe, and quite a few farmers. It is said that the writing of the twelve-article constitution took only eighteen days because the new lawmakers had to get back to the business of farming. On June 29, the document was finished, largely copied from the U.S. Constitution and the constitutions of surrounding states. The total cost of the convention and new constitution was a bargain—about $10,000.

On August 5, 1816, Indiana held its first general election with Jonathan Jennings elected the first governor. As the state grew, however, it became apparent that Corydon was a bit out of the way to be state capital. Commissioners were charged with finding a better location. They chose a place almost precisely in the geographic center of the state—Indianapolis.

However, the settlement back then certainly didn't look like a capital city. Little more than a collection of shacks on the White River, the city was then known as the Fall Creek Settlement. The first European settlers of what would become Indianapolis were John, James, and Samuel McCormick. John and his brother built a log cabin on the east bank of the White River in 1820. He lived there with his wife and eight children. John was one of three of the first county commissioners of Marion County, named for Revolutionary War General Francis Marion, nicknamed the "Swamp Fox."

It was in McCormick's home that Indianapolis was chosen as Indiana's new state capital. The engineer who laid out the plans for Indianapolis stayed with McCormick to do his work. On the east bank of the White River in what is now White River State Park is McCormick's Rock, a memorial that commemorates the site of McCormick's cabin.

Now the state legislature had to choose a name for the new capital. That honor went to Judge Jeremiah Sullivan, who invented the name by joining "Indiana" with "polis," the Greek word for city. Then came the hard work of making the small settlement into a fitting state capital. Not everyone was sure it would happen. The new capital was a scraggly village. Its only cleared street was full of tree stumps. The houses were scattered about the deep woods and could only be reached by cow paths. With the final decision to bring the capital here, Indianapolis began to show signs of permanency.

Alexander Ralston, who had helped Charles L'Enfant design Washington, D.C., was chosen to bring order to the heavily wooded site. He designed a city modeled after Washington. He laid out Indianapolis in a circular pattern based on a square mile because that was as large as he thought the struggling city would ever become. Ralston's 1821 plan called for four diagonal streets radiating out from the center like spokes on a wagon wheel.

At the center, on a wooded knoll circled by a wide street, would sit the governor's mansion. Completed in 1827, the mansion cost $6,500 during the term of Governor James B. Ray, but the governor's wife refused to move into the home because of its lack of privacy. Having the first family's dirty laundry hung out for all to see on the public square was not a happy prospect. No governor ever lived in the mansion, and it was eventually demolished in 1857. Later, Governor's Circle became known as Monument Circle when the magnificent Soldiers and Sailors Monument was completed on the site in 1901.

At first, it seemed as though doubters might be proven right. A malaria outbreak, caused by mosquito infestation around Pogue's Run and White River, hit the settlement in 1821 and again in 1822, claiming many lives. But by the end of 1822, the town had a gristmill, two sawmills, three groceries, two mercantile houses, several small workshops, and seven taverns.

Indianapolis was ready to become the capital. The exhausted group that trekked from Corydon finally arrived with bells on. Mary

Anderson Naylor recalled in her writings that one of the wagon men "had a fashion of putting bells on his horses whenever we came near a town. So we went into the seat of government with fine, large, strong horses strung with bells, all ringing. The sound brought the good people out to stare at us."

The first session of the General Assembly convened there in January 1825. The move proved to be a good decision. Indianapolis thrived and is now the twelfth largest city in the nation. Corydon also went on to prosper. Located less than thirty miles west of Louisville, Corydon is a lovely county seat that proudly preserves its heritage. In the central square stands the limestone building used by the early legislators.

As for that shady elm tree where Indiana's constitution was drafted, it became the most photographed tree in Indiana and a trademark of Corydon. A local chapter of Daughters of the American Revolution was organized in Corydon in 1908 and took its name from the tree: the Hoosier Elm Chapter. With its majestic spot on a riverbank, the tree became a popular place for group pictures, even wedding photographs. In the early 1920s, a doctor exchanged vows with his bride in an open-top touring car under the shade of the Constitution Elm.

At its peak, the tree was fifty feet tall with a trunk diameter of five feet and a spread of 132 feet. When a bad spate of Dutch elm disease hit Indiana, Constitution Elm began to show signs of dying. Despite efforts to save it, the tree died in the summer of 1924. In August of 1925, all the dead limbs were removed and only the large massive trunk was left standing. The stump was preserved and a brick shrine was built over it.

The wood of the giant elm was saved for posterity. Cross sections from its massive limbs were given to museums, colleges, universities, and libraries throughout Indiana. Bits were made into gavels and also sold as souvenirs, so Constitution Elm still lives on in many places.

THE FALL CREEK MASSACRE

1824

Two families of Indians decided to go hunting for game and valuable animal pelts near present-day Pendleton in Madison County. The Indians camped along Fall Creek where animals were plentiful. At the time, Indiana was still part of the frontier. Although the Indians had ceded the land to the United States, there were few white settlers as yet, and Indians often returned to their native land to hunt or fish.

Gathered at the Indian camp on March 22, 1824, were an older Seneca named Ludlow—a venerable chief said to be a friend to the white man—another man named Mingo, three women, and four children—two boys and two girls all under ten years old.

Thomas Harper, a frontiersman who lived in the area, disliked Indians and wanted to get rid of the small Seneca group. Harper was reported to have said "it is no worse to kill an Indian than to kill a deer." A hunter himself, Harper also saw an easy chance to get some animal pelts.

To join him in his attack, Harper persuaded his brother-in-law, John T. Bridge Sr., Bridge's seventeen-year-old son, John Bridge Jr., James Hudson, and Andrew Sawyer.

As a ploy to catch the Indians off guard, the men approached the campsite and asked for help in tracking down some horses they said had escaped from Harper's farm. The friendly Indians agreed to help, and the two older Indians headed into the woods with the white men. Harper and Ludlow went in one direction, Hudson and Mingo in another. The two white men fell behind the Indians as they were walking and shot them in the back.

Returning to the camp, Harper and Hudson along with their cohorts slaughtered the rest of the Indians. One of the boys was only wounded, but reportedly Sawyer banged the child's head against a log until he was dead. The men then robbed the camp and returned home with their loot.

The next day, a nearby farmer found the murderous scene and reported it to officials. News had already spread that the peaceful Indians had been killed, and settlers were worried that other Indians would seek revenge. That didn't seem to bother the murderers, who bragged of their vile deed. After all, no one had ever been arrested for killing an Indian.

But within a week, these men were in custody, except for Harper, who had taken off with his stolen goods and reportedly left the territory, maybe bound for Ohio. Despite a reward of $225—a fortune at the time—Harper seemed to have vanished and was never seen again. To ease a tense situation, a community leader named William Conner and an Indian agent named John Johnston went to local Indian villages and apologized for the atrocity. The men had been arrested and were going to pay for their crimes, the Indians were assured. Because of that, the threat of Indian retaliation was removed and the Indians—along with the rest of the nation—waited to see the alleged murderers face justice.

The four men were tried in Madison County Court in front of a circuit court panel with three judges: Samuel Holliday, Adam Winsell, and William Wick. Senator James Noble was the prosecutor, and Governor William Hendricks instructed the court to show no mercy on the men if they were convicted.

James Hudson was tried first and found guilty. A major point of emotional evidence in the trial was the display of the Indian clothing, soaked with blood. Hudson was sentenced to be hanged on December 1, 1824. The verdict and sentencing were very significant to the new nation. It marked the first time any white man in the United States had been sentenced to death for killing a Native American.

Hudson appealed his verdict but it was upheld. Awaiting execution, Hudson escaped from jail on November 15 and hid in a hollow log in the woods. After suffering frostbite and dehydration, Hudson was recaptured ten days later when he left his hiding place to find water. While he was at large, Hudson's execution date had been changed to January.

When execution day arrived on January 12, 1825, a large crowd turned out to watch the historic event. Among the spectators were several relatives of the Indian victims. No longer able to walk because of his frostbite, Hudson had to be carried to a wagon where he sat on his own coffin for the short trip to the gallows.

Before he was hanged, Hudson said he was sorry and had been led astray by his no-good friends. The condemned man asked a minister who had visited him in jail to preach a short sermon and requested that his body be given to his friends for a proper funeral. Despite his request that they attend the execution, Hudson's wife and young children had returned home to Ohio before the hanging. Hudson's body was taken down from the gallows and buried the next day in the village cemetery north of the falls.

The next trials went quickly. On Tuesday, May 9, 1825, Andrew Sawyer was found guilty and sentenced to death. On Wednesday, John Bridge Jr. was found guilty and sentenced to death. On Thursday, John Bridge Sr. was found guilty and sentenced to death. All three men were scheduled to be hanged on June 3, 1825.

However, several jury members and law officials, as well as a minister and many community members, asked that the young Bridge be pardoned because of his age and because his father and uncle had undue negative influence on him. A petition was circulated for his freedom. On the day of the execution, the young Bridge watched as his father and his uncle were put to death. Next it was his turn. And no pardon had been received from the governor.

Perhaps to stall for time and to comfort the condemned teen, a minister preached a sermon before Bridge was led to the gallows. The hangman's noose was lowered over his neck and it looked as though the young man would surely hang. Suddenly, a cheer went up from the back of the crowd.

One of the state's most flamboyant chief executives, Governor James Brown Ray, galloped up on his horse and looked the condemned boy in the face. Only he, the governor announced, had the power to save Bridges. He then dramatically proclaimed, "You are pardoned."

The horror of his incarceration, seeing his father and uncle hanged, and almost dying himself was said to have so unhinged the young man that Bridge collapsed and was "hopelessly deranged" for the rest of his life.

A stone marker commemorates the hanging of the men who committed the Fall Creek Massacre. Located in Fall Creek Park in Pendleton, the stone is inscribed with the words THREE WHITE MEN WERE HUNG HERE IN 1825 FOR KILLING INDIANS. Author Jessamyn West later used the incident as the basis for her 1975 novel *The Massacre at Fall Creek*.

GOLD DISCOVERED IN BROWN COUNTY

1830s

When John Richards panned some gold flecks in a creek near Nashville in the 1830s, he set off a flurry of excitement. Folks flush with gold fever hunkered down over streams with names like Bear Creek, Lick Creek, and Bean Blossom Creek. A few lucky ones panned out a dollar or two of gold per day. The most valuable nugget found was worth $1.10.

Outfits with bulky equipment rushed to Brown County to strike it rich. Richards leased out a stretch of his farm to some prospectors. They constructed a long flume of oak timber for gold washing. But just as it was completed, a heavy rain swelled the stream and the flume was demolished.

That ended that venture.

Gold fever surfaced again off and on over the years. In 1875 the Brown County Mining Co. was created with 2,000 shares owned by local people. The company did not average more than 25 cents of gold a day. The efforts didn't last long. None of the commercial operations proved to be successful.

Ironically, the village of Nashville was sitting on a gold mine the whole time. Folks just weren't aware of it.

Mother Nature had blessed Nashville with scenic beauty that attracts artists, tourists, and residents.

Of course, Brown County had been around for a long time before artists discovered it. Back in the early 1800s, the first non-Indian settlers came to Brown County. They came looking for rich farmland and stands of good timber. They found rich deposits of clay, deep quarries of stone, and abundant salt licks.

They traveled in open drawn wagons, on foot, and horseback over the treacherous Indian trails. Most of them came from Kentucky, Tennessee, Ohio, Virginia, and the Carolinas. Many of them deliberately chose to live in the rugged country around Nashville because they felt at home in the hills.

Others had fled from low, swampy land and had come to the hills to escape malaria. The first ridges, peaks, and streams were given imaginative names—Pike's Peak, Bear Wallow, Gnaw Bone, Rag Shake Holler, Greasy Creek, Milk Sick Bottom, and Booger Hollow.

William Elkins was the first pioneer to settle with his family in what became Brown County. He came from Pulaski County in Kentucky in 1820. William Snider was one of the earliest settlers in what became the county seat of Nashville. He arrived in 1824 from Kentucky, cleared some land, and built a log cabin.

He and his wife, Jane Evans, had separated before he left Kentucky. Snider, known as "Kentucky Bill," decided his daughter Eliza, born in 1823, should join him in Indiana. In 1828, history records, Kentucky Bill made a trip back to Kentucky and kidnapped his child. He made the entire round-trip by horseback. On the return trip, five-year-old Eliza sat on a pillow in front of her father's saddle. Snider held her with one hand and guided the horse with the other hand.

When Brown County was organized in 1826, Snider and seven other men donated a tract of fifty acres for the site of the courthouse, the jail, and the village of Nashville. County agent Banner Brummet laid out the town in August 1836. He called it Jacksonburg in honor of Andrew Jackson. Because Indiana already had a Jacksonburg, the name was later changed to Nashville as a tribute to Brummet's former old home in Nashville, Tennessee.

In 1872 the town was incorporated. And by 1880, the streets boasted neat white houses. Each house was enclosed by a white-washed picket or board fence to keep out the cows and horses that roamed the streets at night.

In the early 1890s, an artist wandered into the Brown County hills, setting off a migration that would forever change the future of Nashville.

Fred A. Hetherington thought he had found a painter's paradise. Although he never settled in Nashville, Hetherington tried to spread the news. Scenic vistas, fields of wildflowers, quiet overlooks where wild animals and magnificent birds seemed to pose, abandoned barns, and huge forests provided inspiration for artists.

But it wasn't until Adolph Shulz and Theodore Clement Steele arrived that the artists' colony was formed. Reading about Brown County in a Chicago newspaper, Shulz decided to check it out for himself. Printed in August 1900, the newspaper article extolled the scenic beauty of the hills and hollows, the quaint log cabins, and the stalwart people.

A Wisconsin native and Chicago artist, Shulz thought he would see if the article was indeed correct. Arriving in Indianapolis, Shulz caught a train to Columbus and rented a horse and buggy to travel around Brown County. "A sense of peace and loveliness never before experienced came over me," he wrote. Shulz vowed to return again as soon as possible.

In June 1907, Shulz and a friend struck out from Martinsville for a two-week hike in southern Indiana. Shulz found his way to a place down the road in Belmont where famed artist Steele was building a home known as the "House of the Singing Winds." A member of the "Hoosier Group" of artists and the "dean of Indiana artists," Steele was the first known artist to live in Brown County. Arising each morning by 4:00, Steele would grab his supplies and begin his long hike into the woods to capture the first glimpse of dawn on his canvas. His wife's flower gardens were among his favorite subjects, and one of his last works was an unfinished painting of peonies from her garden. The painting still rests on the same easel today at the T.C. Steele State Historic Site, just as it was when Steele passed away in 1926.

With the construction of the Illinois Central railroad in 1907, the Brown County area became more hospitable and accessible. During the summer of 1908, there were at least twenty-five artists painting in and near Nashville, including Shulz and his artist wife, Ada Walter Shulz. The number increased steadily until more than sixty artists were spending summers working in Nashville.

Other artists discovered Brown County. Some came to stay: Frank K. Phoenix, Wilson Irvine, Harry L. Engle, Adam Emory Albright, Rudolph Ingerle, Karl Kraft, John Hafen, and Mary Murray Vawter. Many of them set up studios—Gustave Baumann on the first floor of the Odd Fellows building, Dale P. Bessire at an apple orchard on the edge of town, L. O. Griffith in an old creamery building, and William Vawter above the old Star Grocery store.

V. J. Cariani built a home. C. Curry Bohm moved to a farm. Photographer Frank Hohenberger recorded life with his camera, and political satirist Kin Hubbard created his "Abe Martin" cartoons. Originally from Indianapolis, Marie Goth moved to Brown County in 1923 with her sister Genevieve. An excellent painter of portraits,

Goth always insisted that her subjects come to her studio for a sitting. By the time she died, Goth had painted several prominent Indiana residents and was the only woman in Indiana to paint an official portrait of a governor.

After her death, Goth's property, most of her money, and many of her paintings were donated to the Brown County Art Guild. Those early artists were the forerunners of the craftspeople and artists in the Brown County arts colony.

By October of 1926, the first art gallery was opened in Nashville. It was an immediate success. A steady stream of traffic raised such dust on the rough roads that drivers kept their lights on to prevent collisions, local lore says.

Another big boost came in 1930 when the establishment of Brown County State Park opened the area even more to the outside world. In 1933 Hohenberger described Nashville to a magazine writer: "When I moved here, this was a place with only about 300 population, with two groceries, a livery stable, a drugstore, and a boardinghouse; a village far off the railroad with no industries, dependent on the trade of the hill folks."

In his diary, he pictured Nashville as a place with unpaved streets, wood-burning stoves, individual water supplies, and helpful but curious neighbors. It was, he said, "a village nestling in the valley of peace," where he found "the restfulness that brings inspiration."

Tourists who had heard about the beauty of Brown County began making pilgrimages to see the hills, forests, and streams and to buy the artists' works. Roads began to develop. So popular did it become that the *Milwaukee Journal* reported in 1949 that Nashville had the most important art colony between New England and New Mexico.

Today, visitors come to the place that holds dear its legendary past. An unofficial estimate notes that at least eight hundred artists live in Brown County, and Nashville (population 826) is chock-full of interesting shops, lodgings, and restaurants. Artists' work ranges across painting, pottery, weaving, photography, writing, carving, jewelry making, and other arts.

Artists and visitors speak in hushed awe of the "blue haze" that settles over the Brown County hills. The dramatic mix of light and mist casts a soft glow that beckons painters, photographers, and nature lovers to pull off the path and enjoy the magical scene.

TRAIL OF DEATH

1838

The scene was terrifying. Soldiers fired their guns to capture the unarmed Potawatomi Indian village. Father Petit's chapel was closed. Soldiers scattered in all directions to round up Indians within a thirty- to fifty-mile radius. Three Indian chiefs—Menominee, Black Wolf, and Pepinawa—were chained and put in jail wagons.

The infamous forced relocation of the Potawatomi was about to begin. On September 4, 1838, nearly 900 Potawatomi Indians were corralled by U.S. soldiers and marched at gunpoint for 61 days over 665 hard miles. The treacherous journey started in Plymouth, Indiana, and slowly traveled across the great prairie of Illinois, over the Mississippi River, through Missouri, and on to Kansas.

On November 4, 1838, the imprisoned group arrived at the end of the trail in Osawatomie, Kansas. Typhoid fever, thirst, hunger, rotten meat, and the stress of the forced march caused so many deaths that the route became known as the Trail of Death.

History records that 859 Potawatomi started the journey. Less than 700 finished it. Not all of the 150 left died since many escaped or straggled behind. But the trail is strewn with the graves of more than 40 individuals, mostly children and old folks.

Taking place at the same time, the Cherokee Trail of Tears is more widely known because of the astounding numbers: 16,000 Cherokee were removed from the Smoky Mountains and forced to walk to Oklahoma. More than 4,000 died.

Asking to accompany his Potawatomi congregation on their torturous journey through the Trail of Death, young Father Benjamin Marie Petit said Mass every day and baptized babies who died shortly after they were born. In his words, the innocent babies "with their first step passed from earthy exile to their heavenly sojourn." Father Petit also kept a journal of the devastating march. He, too, lost his life as a result of the hardships he endured. Exhausted by his strenuous experience and weakened by successive attacks of fever and open sores, Father Petit died in St. Louis on February 10, 1939. He was not quite twenty-nine years old.

The confrontation between the Potawatomi and the U.S. government had been building for quite some time. When white settlers first came to the frontier that later became Indiana, the Potawatomi lived in relative peace with their new neighbors. The government of Indiana, however, was eager to open up the northern parts of the state for settlers and development.

In 1830 the federal government passed the Indian Removal Act. The goal of the government was to push Indians from the populated east to the remote and unpopulated lands west of the Mississippi. The Potawatomi were tribes living around the southern edge of Lake Michigan in Michigan and Indiana. In October 1832, treaties were signed at Tippecanoe on the Wabash in which the Indians ceded most of their remaining land in northwestern and north-central Indiana. In exchange, the Potawatomi were given land in Potawatomi County, Kansas, and yearly annuities.

More treaties were signed over the next four years that stripped the Potawatomi of their land in Indiana. These treaties were known as the Whiskey Treaties because whiskey was often given to get the Indians to sign.

But Chief Menominee and his band at Twin Lakes, Indiana, refused to sign the treaties.

Chief Menominee was a Catholic convert as were many of those residing in the village. Menominee had invited the Black Robes, as the priests were often called, to come to his village and construct a mission church. That was done in 1834 and 1935. Menominee instructed his people to abstain from alcohol and led them in worship and prayer twice daily.

After the Treaty of Yellow River was signed in August 1836, the deadline for the tribe to peacefully leave their land was set for August 5, 1836. Nearly the entire Potawatomi nation left peacefully for their new land in Kansas. All that remained was Chief Menominee and his tribe at their Twin Lakes village near Plymouth, Indiana. The deadline came and went. The village refused to move.

Finally, Indiana Governor David Wallace ordered General John Tipton to use the state militia to forcibly remove Chief Menominee and his tribe. On August 30, Tipton and about one hundred soldiers surrounded Twin Lakes and captured the Indians, burning their homes and crops to discourage them from trying to return. The Indians were marched in line with soldiers on both sides. Reports said that six-year-old Billy Ward followed his Indian friends, wanting to go along, but his mother caught him and took him home.

When the mile-long line of Indians was herded through Rochester, sympathetic white settlers turned out and gave them hoecakes to take on the trip. In his diary, the army's enrolling agent Jesse C. Douglas noted that a child fell off a wagon and was crushed by the wheels. "Will probably die," Douglas wrote.

Father Petit described it as "a scene of desolation with sick and dying people on all sides . . . We soon found ourselves on the grand prairie of Illinois, under a burning sun and without shade from one camp to another. They are as vast as the ocean and the eye seeks in vain for a tree. Not a drop of water can be found there—it was a veritable torture for our poor sick, some of whom died each day from weakness and fatigue."

The group arrived at Osawatomie, Kansas, on November 4, 1838, the end of the trail. Winter was coming on and there were supposed to be houses ready for the Indians. But no houses had been built for them. The Potawatomi built wigwams and survived the winter as best they could. In 1847 they were again moved to a reservation north of Topeka.

After his death in a Jesuit seminary in St. Louis, Father Petit was buried in an old cemetery at Seventh Street and St. Charles Avenue. When the cemetery was moved in 1856 to make way for downtown St. Louis, Petit's body was returned to Indiana. His remains rest under the Log Chapel at the University of Notre Dame in South Bend. Petit is remembered by the Catholic Church as a martyr of charity because of his service to the Potawatomi.

Today a Trail of Death Regional Historic Trail is complete with seventy-four historical markers tracing the march from Indiana to Kansas. Visitors are asked to travel the trail, stop and read the markers, and say a prayer for peace for all people.

SANTA CLAUS COMES TO TOWN

1852

A long time ago, a group of people lived in a small Southern Indiana community known as Santa Fe. When the Christmas season rolled around, the townspeople were so excited that for the first time they would have their own post office to mail their greetings and gifts.

Unfortunately, a big official envelope arrived notifying residents that Indiana already had a "Santa Fe." The town couldn't get a post office until it had a new name. The people thought and thought, but every name they came up with seemed already to be taken. So the town that was formed mostly by German settlers in the late 1840s became known by the sad moniker of the "Nameless Town."

Determined to finally get their name and post office, the citizens of Nameless Town decided to discuss the matter at the town's 1852 Christmas Eve celebration. Gathered around the potbellied, wood-burning stove in the little log church, folks suggested this name and that. They even mentioned naming the town Wyttenbach after the popular circuit-riding preacher, the Reverend Christian Wyttenbach, who had just preached the holiday service. Although he was honored, the reverend respectfully declined. He didn't even live there.

Suddenly, a cold December gust blew open the door of the church. In the distance could be heard the faint sound of sleigh bells ringing through the quiet winter night. It was quite puzzling since there was no one around for miles. Everyone was in the tiny church.

But the children were not puzzled. The voice of a small child excitedly rang out, "It's Santa Claus, it's Santa Claus." The congregation had its answer. Nameless Town became Santa Claus.

And the name of Santa Claus, Indiana—along with its distinctive postmark—has become known around the world. On May 21, 1856, the U.S. Post Office Department approved a post office for the newly renamed town of Santa Claus, Indiana. The tiny Hoosier town is the only place in America named after the Jolly Ol' Elf, and every year—well, practically, every day—they go crazy for Christmas.

Come Christmas time, an estimated 500,000 pieces of mail find their way to the tiny Spencer County post office. During the rest of the year, about 13,000 pieces of mail are processed each month—as much mail as the post office processes each day during the Christmas season.

As the only "Santa Claus Post Office" in the world, the Hoosier office offers a different picture postmark each holiday season since 1983. The postmark is designed by a local high school art student each year, as part of an annual contest.

Over the years, Santa Claus has become more than the popular post office and unique postmark. It has evolved into a year-round attraction anchored by the world's first theme park, Holiday World. How the amusement park ended up there is another interesting tale.

It was before World War II when Evansville industrialist Louis J. Koch planned to create the park as a retirement project. He was always troubled by the fact that the tiny Hoosier hamlet of Santa Claus was visited by children around the country who were ultimately disappointed when they found out that Santa was not there to chat with them.

With nine children of his own, Koch loved children, holidays, and celebrations. World War II forced Koch to wait until 1946 to open his dream park. Known as Santa Claus Land, the attraction originally featured a toy shop, toy displays, themed children's rides, a restaurant, and, of course, Santa Claus.

Over the decades, Santa Claus Land grew and flourished. Halloween and the Fourth of July sections were added in 1984, and the name was changed to Holiday World. Thanksgiving is the newest holiday section to be included. Larger rides were added, including the popular Raging Rapids white-water raft ride, Splashin' Safari Water Park, Monsoon Lagoon, and The Raven wooden roller coaster. In all, Holiday World features one hundred acres of rides, shows, games, and attractions.

Then along came another part of the legend. A man named Jim Yellig moved to the Indiana town from Chicago. About the same time, *Ripley's Believe It Or Not* featured a segment on the Santa Claus Post Office, and the result was a flood of visitors and mail addressed simply to "Santa Claus."

To add some holiday cheer in the 1930s, Yellig began visiting the Santa Claus Post Office in his Santa costume to entertain the children and tourists who stopped by to visit. Born in 1895 in nearby Mariah Hill, Yellig began his career as Santa Claus when he was in the Navy. In 1914 his ship pulled into port in New York so the crew could celebrate Christmas.

Yellig and his shipmates decided to throw a Christmas party for the poor and underprivileged children who lived in Brooklyn Navy Yard. The sailors pitched in a dollar a piece for gifts for the children.

Since Yellig once told his shipmates that he lived in a small town near Santa Claus, he was naturally elected to play Old St. Nick at the party. Yellig looked at the happy youngsters and made a pledge: If he made it through the war and returned home, he would try to keep bringing the joy of Christmas to youngsters as Santa Claus.

Living in the town of Santa Claus made it easy for Yellig to keep that promise. In his volunteer role at the post office, Yellig also pitched in to help answer some of the mail that was pouring in. It soon became a full-time project for Yellig, his wife, and the Santa Claus American Legion. Yellig also found the perfect niche when Santa Claus Land opened. He was hired to become the park's first Santa Claus, a role he enjoyed until his death in 1984.

His daughter, Patricia Yellig Koch, recalls that her father didn't just "play" Santa Claus. When he put on the suit, he was Santa Claus.

Which brings us to the magical tale of Patricia Koch's marriage. Notice that last name? The daughter of Santa Claus at Holiday World married the son of the Holiday World owner. And Koch is carrying on the traditions of both her father and her father-in-law.

Records show that the first person to answer the children's letters to Santa was the Santa Claus postmaster, James Martin, in the year 1914. The community has never missed a year since. In 1974 the nonprofit organization Santa's Elves Inc. was formed to ensure that postage costs are provided each year for children's letters from Santa. Up to 10,000 letters are answered each year by Santa's Elves, assisted by the Christmas Lake Village Garden Club, local senior citizens, and other Yuletide volunteers. Every letter is opened and answered so no child will be disappointed.

Letters written in foreign languages are sent to the monks at nearby St. Meinrad Archabbey and the Sisters of St. Benedict at the Monastery Immaculate Conception in Ferdinand to be answered in the children's own language.

The town itself has special holiday events and names that reflect the Santa Claus heritage. There's Christmas Lake Village, a residential community covering over two thousand acres and three lakes with five hundred acres set aside for recreation. There's also Santa Claus Hardware, Kringle's Kleaners, Santa's Lodge, St. Nick's Restaurant, Frosty's Pizza, Santa Claus Car Care, Ho Ho Ho Video, Holly Plaza, Lake Rudolph Campground, and much more.

The town, with a population of about twelve hundred, has streets with names like Silver Bell Terrace, Candy Cane Lane, Reindeer Circle, and Prancer Drive. Local fire trucks are dubbed Rudolph, Dasher, and Blitzen.

A gigantic Santa Claus statue welcomes visitors. Twenty-two feet high and weighing over forty tons, the granite Santa Claus statue has a special base in the shape of the Star of Bethlehem with its principal point showing the way east to the land of the true Christmas story.

To showcase its heritage, the small community of Santa Claus has a free museum where visitors can learn how the town got its name, how Holiday World was created, and why the place continues to thrive. As townsfolk say, they celebrate Christmas every day.

STUDEBAKERS
START BUILDING WAGONS

1852

On a cold day in February 1852, the Studebaker brothers opened their new wagon building/blacksmith business. Then they waited. Their only customer that first day was a man who wanted his horse shod with two shoes. The brothers did a quick and excellent job. They earned 25 cents. That was it for the whole day.

After all, blacksmiths and wagon builders were common in those times. Setting up shop in South Bend, Indiana, may have seemed like a good idea, but many other entrepreneurs had come to the area hoping to make a living as well.

Within a few days, though, more customers came to the new Studebaker shop. The man who had his horse shod had spread the word that the Studebakers did good work and charged a fair price. It took weeks, however, before the first customer appeared inquiring about having a wagon built. The man wanted a simple farm wagon. The Studebakers obliged. A week later, the buyer plunked down $175 and drove off in a green and red wagon that made folks stop and stare in admiration. Painted on the sides and back in yellow was the name Studebaker.

That was the beginning of a company whose name and products would span the centuries. From the horse-drawn era to the roaring automobiles, the Studebaker name would mean quality on wheels. The Studebaker brothers lived up to their motto of delivering more than you promise.

Back then, of course, such horseless contraptions as automobiles were far from people's minds. Wagons were the way to go, and the Studebakers quickly gained a reputation for producing the best in the business. At their shop, the Studebakers saw wagon trains coming from the east and going west, many of them heading to California and its promise of strike-it-rich gold.

The two Studebaker brothers—Clem and Henry—were doing all right with their smithy and wagon building business. But a third brother, John, decided that his future lay in California. With no money, the twenty-year-old made a wagon and bartered it, along with his skills as a driver, for passage on a wagon train bound for the gold fields. In 1853 the caravan of eighty-five men set off for California. John's mother kissed him goodbye and sent him off with a Bible, three suits of clothes, and a belt into which she had sewn some money.

For five grueling months, the wagon train slowly made its way west. When he hit Placerville, California, John Studebaker realized that his fortune wasn't in gold but in building the wagons that gold miners needed. Although he had never made a wheelbarrow before, John was not afraid to try, and before long the Studebaker name was well known for being a quality wheelbarrow manufacturer.

Meanwhile, back in South Bend, Clem and Henry were climbing up the business ladder. In 1857 the brothers made their first fancy carriage. South Bend was no longer a pioneer town. Women and their families now wanted spiffy carriages for church and social events.

Then came an unexpected boon. The Studebakers were offered a contract to build one hundred wagons for the U.S. government. Of course, they took the huge contract. But then Clem and Henry were faced with a problem. Anyone knew it took at least three years to season lumber for the best wagon material. Green wood just wouldn't do. So the brothers came up with a new method for curing lumber. They built a drying kiln to age lumber right at their business.

Within ninety days, the Studebakers had fulfilled their contract—three months ahead of schedule. The one hundred wagons were ready for the government to send west. All of a sudden, the Studebaker company had made a gigantic leap into a modern industrial process and large-scale distribution.

What the brothers needed now was more capital to expand and go after other large contracts and more hands to realize their dream. Guess who came riding to their rescue? Reading of their good fortune in letters from home, John Studebaker decided that real money for his family was not in the gold mines but in doing what they did best—building wagons. And South Bend—instead of California— was actually the promised land for the Studebakers. After all, folks were going through the Midwest by the thousands, and everyone, it seemed, needed a wagon of some sort.

Taking the $8,000 he had made building wheelbarrows, John returned to South Bend. For the times, he had gotten rich, but John had tried his hand at mining gold only once. John arrived back in South Bend in 1858.

Henry was not well. Working in the smithy forge had been hard on his health, so he sold his part of the business to his younger brother John for $3,000 and became a farmer. Local lore also says that John wanted out of the business because he saw war looming on the horizon and he didn't agree with providing wagons to help fight the war. John was right. When the Civil War hit, the U.S. Army needed even more wagons. By 1868, annual Studebaker sales had reached $350,000. That same year, the Studebaker brothers formed the Studebaker Brothers Manufacturing Company with Clem as president, John as treasurer, and younger brother Peter as secretary. A few years later, youngest brother Jacob was added, put in charge of the carriage factory.

Carriages were a big thing then. A wealthy man might pay $20,000 for a carriage with red wheels, gold-plated lamps, and seating for a dozen preening passengers. Heck, even the President of the United States, William Henry Harrison, himself from Indiana, ordered a full set of Studebaker carriages and harnesses for the White House in 1889. The Harrison Administration paid $7,075 for five carriages, three sets of harnesses, and related accessories for the vehicles. The coaches were simple in design with silver and ebony trimmings rather than fancier gilt, and they bore no formal insignias. The carriages were well suited to Harrison's unpretentious nature.

Between 1887 and 1917, the Studebaker brothers died, with John being the last to go. However, their sons and sons-in-law were active in the family business and ready to help it move forward. In 1895 John's son-in-law Fred Fish had seen the need for the company to develop a practice horseless carriage. In 1902 Studebaker started building electric automobiles, soon switching to gasoline power.

By 1915, Studebaker was building more than 45,000 cars annually, fueled by a growing public passion for the contraptions. The primitive motorcars were expensive but they were catching on. The wagons were now only a sideline. Within a few short years, the wagons would be gone altogether. The last Studebaker wagon was built in 1920.

When World War II erupted, the Studebaker company again got government contracts, only this time for trucks, Flying Fortress airplane engines, and other war supplies. When the war ended, other car companies went back to producing warmed-over prewar models. Not so the Studebakers. They introduced new styling for the 1947 wraparound rear-windowed Starlight Coupe. Exciting 1950 models showcased the famous "bullet nose" styling while 1951 marked the popular new Studebaker V8.

In 1954 Studebaker merged with Packard, which proved disastrous. Studebaker lost $43 million in 1956, and Packard disappeared altogether after 1958. Rebounding in 1959, Studebaker introduced the compact and successful Lark. However, the success was short-lived and financial problems surfaced once again. The Studebaker Avanti debuted in 1963, but in December of 1963, Studebaker closed its South Bend plant. Production continued through March 1966 at a Hamilton, Ontario, Canada plant. A blue and white 1966 Cruiser marked the end of 114 years of Studebaker vehicle production.

But the Studebaker name is still a big part of South Bend. The Studebaker National Museum draws visitors wanting to hear the story of the five brothers and to see some of the wagons they created that parallel the history of the United States. Among the treasures on display are about seventy vehicles, including a Conestoga wagon, a 1902 electric Studebaker, and the carriage that Abraham Lincoln took to Ford Theatre in Washington, D.C., on the evening of April 14, 1865, the night of his assassination.

JOHN HUNT MORGAN'S RAID

1863

His name struck terror in the hearts of Hoosiers. And that was exactly what he wanted.

Confederate General John Hunt Morgan and his troops of two thousand stormed Indiana. The raiders rampaged on horseback through southeastern Indiana over a period of six days from July 8 to July 13, 1863. In all, Morgan's troops hit three states—Kentucky, Indiana, and Ohio—on their twenty-five-day, thousand-mile raid.

Morgan's raid through southern Indiana, also known as the Great Raid of 1863, was the only major military activity in Indiana during the Civil War. Morgan's goal was to stage a series of diversionary raids to distract the Union army's attention away from Confederate forces in Tennessee. Morgan terrorized the people of Indiana. They didn't know where he was going to hit or what he was going to do next. And, in many cases, the rumors were worse than the facts.

About twenty Hoosiers were killed during Morgan's raid and another twenty-four were wounded. Militarily, Morgan didn't accomplish much. But he did wonders for the morale of the Confed eracy and inflicted a lot of damage on Indiana.

Morgan's Raiders crossed the Ohio River aboard two confiscated steamboats into Indiana at Bradenburg, Kentucky. It took all day to ferry the men, horses, and artillery across the river. On July 9, 1863, Morgan's Raiders arrived at Corydon. Waiting for them was the Indiana Home Guard—an inexperienced group of about four hundred farmers and businessmen who attempted to ward off the invaders long enough for Union reinforcements to arrive. The Hoosier forces opened fire from behind a breastwork of logs and repelled the raiders' first attack.

But the Confederates flanked the defenders on both wings. Morgan's men further frightened the people of Corydon when the raiders set up a cannon and fired into the town. The only Civil War battle fought on Indiana soil, the Battle of Corydon lasted less than an hour. Four Hoosiers were killed, several wounded, 355 were captured, and the rest escaped. Eleven Confederates were killed and forty wounded.

All the Indiana soldiers were released after they promised not to fight again. Entering Corydon, the raiders plundered and looted stores and shops, collecting more than $2,000 in tribute before leaving the town late in the day.

The Battle of Corydon Memorial Park, just south of town, marks the site where the Home Guard fought off Morgan's Raiders. Listed on the National Register of Historic Places, the five-acre park in the one-time state capital has a commemorative cannon, a stone memorial listing battle casualties, and a small log cabin representative of area homes of that period.

After leaving Corydon, Morgan's Raiders headed north and east, passing through the communities of Palmyra, Salem, Vienna, and Lexington, destroying property and looting as they went.

The people of Indiana didn't know if there were two thousand raiders or six thousand or eight thousand or ten thousand. Morgan and his raiders didn't come in one nice long column, so it was hard to count the exact number. Morgan's Raiders didn't bring supplies with them, so they had to find horses and food. To get what they needed, the men would ransack merchants and homes. To find enough food and horses, the raiders had to spread out. They cut a swath about ten to twenty miles wide.

Some Hoosiers at Salem thought they might be able to defeat Morgan and his men. When they saw the southern cavalrymen coming up the road toward the courthouse, however, the local men immediately scattered.

Morgan's men looted the town and, for the price of $1,000 from each miller, promised not to destroy the mills. Before the rebels left Salem, they burned the depot, three railroad cars, the water tower, and two railroad bridges. They then headed east to Canton where they wrecked more railroad tracks and tore down telegraph wires.

By the night of July 10, the raiders had reached Vienna. Still drunk from quantities of whiskey they had downed in Salem, the unruly men began ransacking farmers' homes. Searching for money, they ripped up bedding and carpets and broke clocks and mirrors.

Along with taking food and replacement horses, the raiders began to steal and destroy just for the sake of doing it. One trooper was said to have carried off a birdcage with three canaries in it. Other raiders took bolts of calico, tied one end to their saddles with the calico streaming behind them as they rode out of town. In Salem, they stole ice skates. Then they would discard things they didn't want as they went down the road.

The actions of the raiders escalated as they tore through Indiana. The mood was almost mass hysteria with the men destroying as much as they stole. Even the raiders later admitted that they had never seen anything like the destructive madness that was unleashed.

As darkness fell, most of the raiders turned toward Lexington, which at that time was the county seat of Scott County. At the cemetery, some elderly men and young boys prepared to defend the town with an old cannon. But on seeing Morgan's troops, they quickly dispersed. Legend has it that one little Lexington girl, afraid the invaders would steal her pony, hid the animal behind a piano in her home.

In the midnight hour of Saturday, July 11, the raiders descended on Dupont in Jefferson County and were able to catch a few hours rest before devouring an early breakfast at the expense of almost every homestead. They stole two thousand hams from Frank Mayfield's meat packing plant and required the village wives to prepare a ham breakfast for them. Tales says the raiders left town with hams dangling from their saddles.

The meat packer's daughter was so outraged and defiant that she gave the Confederates a bold piece of her mind. One Kentucky raider was so awed by her brave spunk that he told her when the war ended, he was going to come back, court her, and marry her. He did, too, and their descendants still live in the area.

The main column continued to Versailles, the seat of Ripley County, which surrendered without a shot being fired. The defending Union Guards were imprisoned in the courthouse and their guns confiscated and broken over the corner edges of the courthouse.

The raiders stole $5,000 from the Ripley County treasury and a group of raiders invaded the local Masonic Lodge and lifted the lodge's silver jewelry. However, Morgan was a mason himself and ordered the men to return the jewels.

The last Indiana county the raiders terrorized was Dearborn. There the raiders cut telegraph wire and burned bridges. On July 13, they crossed the Whitewater River on a heavy oak bridge that spanned the river. Two hours later, the pursuing Union troops came to the smoldering oak bridge. Morgan's Raiders had burned it after crossing the Ohio state line.

Throughout most of the raid, Morgan's column was pursued by a Union cavalry force of four thousand under the command of Brigadier General Edward Hobson. The Confederate soldiers also were pursued by thirteen regiments of twenty thousand men mustered into service under Major General Lew Wallace.

After leaving Indiana, Morgan and his raiders continued a path of destruction across the state of Ohio. The raid ended July 26 with Morgan's capture in northeastern Ohio.

Morgan and his troops had inflicted several million dollars' worth of damage during their three-state raid. By one estimate, the raiders captured and paroled six thousand Northern soldiers, destroyed thirty-four major bridges, demolished railroad tracks in sixty different locations, burned numerous warehouses and depots, and pillaged countless homes and businesses.

Although he was put in maximum security in a prison in Columbus, Ohio, Morgan and six others escaped and made it back to the Confederacy. A little over a year later, on September 4, 1864, Morgan was shot in the back by a Yankee in Greenville, Tennessee. Morgan was thirty-nine years old. He died instantly.

A staunch Union supporter, Indiana paid heavily during the Civil War. Critical to the Union's success because of its rich farmland and agricultural yield, Indiana also contributed a total of 208,367 men to fight and serve in the Union Army and 2,130 in the Union Navy. Most of the soldiers from Indiana were volunteers and many reenlisted at least once. More than 35 percent of those Hoosiers became casualties—24,416 lost their lives in the Civil War and more than 50,000 returned home bearing disfiguring and debilitating wounds and scars.

The last person to be killed in combat during the Civil War was a Hoosier of the 34th Regiment Indiana Infantry. On May 13, 1865, at the Battle of Palmito Ranch on the banks of the Rio Grande in southern Texas, Private John Jay Williams was struck by a sniper's bullet and killed.

EXPLOSION ABOARD THE *ARGOSY*

1865

The Union soldiers had survived some of the worst battles of the Civil War. They had fought at Vicksburg, Chickamauga, Chattanooga, and the Atlanta campaign. They had been with Sherman in his horrific "march to the sea."

Now the battle-weary soldiers were on their way home. About three hundred newly mustered-out veterans of the 70th Ohio Infantry overloaded the commandeered steamer boat, the *Argosy III,* for the trip from Cairo, Illinois, to Cincinnati. Eager to return home and hug their loved ones once again, the battle-scarred soldiers thought they were lucky to have survived the horrendous war. But one of the worst tragedies of their lives was still ahead.

On the afternoon of August 21, 1865, a ferocious storm descended on the steamboat. Buffeted by strong winds and driving rain, the *Argosy* plowed on. The soldiers huddled around the steamer's boiler to stay warm and escape the cold rain. Suddenly, the storm pushed the *Argosy* against the shore. The *Argosy* was blown against rock about eighty miles west of Louisville near the tiny Indiana town of Magnet.

The boat's straining mud drums exploded when the *Argosy* hit the Indiana shore. Mud drums collected sediment from the river water fed into the steam system and were located between the boilers and the hulls. Steam and boiling water sprayed all over the soldiers nearest the engines. Many of the soldiers jumped into the water and survived. But the eleven men closest to the boiler were scalded alive.

The victims—nine members of the 70th Ohio Regiment and an unknown soldier from the 39th Indiana Infantry—were buried in a mass grave. Survivors were plucked from the river by another steamboat and taken to Louisville. The first boat to come to the scene was the original *Argosy,* which also had been pressed into service in the war. A riverboat pilot from nearby Vevay had just purchased the boat at an auction and was on his way home with it. Two more men later died from their injuries in Louisville.

The *Argosy III* was patched and towed to Louisville, where it was repaired and put back into service. Originally built in 1864, the boat steamed area rivers for ten more years before it was dismantled.

That dreadful accident is commemorated in what might be one of the nation's smallest and most overlooked Civil War cemeteries. Near the bank of the Ohio River known as Rono Bottoms, the tiny cemetery sits in a small clearing a half mile down an unnamed gravel road.

No signs mark the commemorative spot in Perry County. Folks searching for the graves often stop in the tiny town of Magnet, with its four houses and one business, Rono's Landing Tavern and Restaurant. The memorial site is about a mile southeast of Magnet along the river road from town. The site is on the landward side of the road and is open to the public. Magnet is about three miles off IN 66.

The burial site might long ago have disappeared in weeds and brambles. But the people of Magnet have made sure the graves are tended and the dead soldiers are not forgotten. In 1965 Clyde Benner made a small clearing in the woods along the gravel road beside the river. He poured a concrete base for ten white headstones given by the federal government. The Indiana Civil War Centennial Commission supplied a Civil War Memorial Grave marker. Benner owned eighty acres of woods fronting the accident site. As a veteran, Benner made it his job to be caretaker for the soldiers the river had left behind.

When Benner was done with his work, the local folks held a dedication service. People dressed in old-timey clothes paid tribute to the fallen soldiers, Benner continued clearing and weeding the gravesite in the grove of poplars, maples, locust, and cottonwood trees until his death in 1985. Then his land was divided among his four daughters and the daughter who drew the lot with the graveyard, Pat Irwin, took over her father's job, adding a split rail fence and some flowers.

Carved into the headstones are the names: Amos Rose, Aaron Fiscus, John McDaniel, George W. McKinney, Hugh T. Taylor, Martin V. B. Long, John Robuck, Albert Rader, John Behrens, and "Unknown U.S. Soldier."

As townspeople like to point out, these men fought for their country, they left behind families, and they should not be forgotten.

FIRST UNITED STATES
TRAIN ROBBERY

1866

On a dark gloomy night in 1866, a band of outlaws lay in wait near a railroad water tank outside Seymour, Indiana. Hidden among firewood stacked beside the track as fuel for the train, the men patiently waited for their prey. Fog from an evening rain helped obscure their hiding place.

Suddenly, a long, low locomotive whistle cut through the night. The men sprang to action. As the glare of the approaching engine illuminated the tracks ahead, the men prepared for their dastardly deed. When the train came to a grinding stop by the water tank, the bandits and three gang members who had boarded the train as passengers in Seymour terrorized the trainmen before making off with $16,000 from a small safe. They were unable to open a larger safe, which some said held $35,000 in gold.

The infamous Reno Gang had just pulled off the first train robbery in U.S. history, that night of October 6, 1866.

Following the Civil War, train robberies were more frequent in the United States than anywhere else in the world. Wide expanses of unsettled country permitted bandits to quickly escape. Lack of adequate security on trains made robberies easier. Robbers could be assured that valuables were on trains, carried by the sitting-duck passengers and in train safes.

Train robberies peaked in 1870. Among the best-known train robbers were the Reno brothers in southern Indiana, the Farringtons in Kentucky and Tennessee, the Daltons in Oklahoma, and the Jesse James gang who wreaked havoc throughout the Midwest. Trying to protect passengers and railroaders as well as stop the huge losses of money, railroad companies hired the Pinkerton National Detective Agency in Chicago. Pinkerton detectives proved quite successful in tracking down their men.

The Reno family had moved to Indiana from Kentucky in 1813. Settling on a farm just north of present-day Seymour, Wilkinson Reno married Julia Ann Freyhafer and started raising a family on his 1,200-acre property. Frank was born in 1837, John in 1838, Simeon in 1843, Clinton in 1847, William in 1848, and Laura in 1851.

The older Reno boys were said to be a handful even as children. Skipping school, shirking chores, and rebelling against attending church and reading the Bible, the older boys were a troublesome bunch. However, next-to-youngest boy Clint didn't want to have anything to do with his brothers' criminal escapades. (A bit of trivia: Clint Reno was the character played by Elvis Presley in his first movie in 1956, *Love Me Tender*. In the movie, Clint stayed home while his brothers went to fight in the Civil War for the Confederate Army.)

In real life, John Reno wrote an autobiography in 1879 claiming that his crime spree began at an early age when he and older brother

Frank would lure travelers passing their farm into crooked card games. John left home as a teen, stole a horse, and moved to New Orleans. Dissatisfied with life on the road, he came back home about a year later, stole some money from his parents, and took off again.

When a series of mysterious fires broke out in the area, the Renos were suspected. For seven years, beginning in 1851, homes and businesses were set ablaze. No one ever discovered the identity of the arsonists. But many people thought they knew and suspicion was definitely pointed toward the Renos.

When the Civil War started, Frank and John discovered they could make money through "bounty jumping." Federal recruiting officers would pay a bounty to any man who enlisted. So the Reno brothers would enlist, pocket the money, and then desert. A while later, they would show up in another area and repeat the scheme. When the draft started, men who were drafted but didn't want to fight in the war could hire someone else to go in their place. The Renos, however, carried the idea a bit further. They would accept the bounty and enlist in the place of some other man, deserting shortly thereafter. Then they would find another man who wanted a soldier to go in his stead and start the process all over again.

Eventually the Renos and their assorted criminal cohorts formed a gang with Frank as the top man and John second in command. Robberies, burglaries, and other crimes in the area escalated, all laid at the feet of the Reno Gang. On August 3, 1865, the *Seymour Times* ran an editorial decrying the lawlessness and noting that vigilantes needed to take matters into their own hands to protect citizens. "Nothing but Lynch law will save the reputation of this place and its citizens," editor J.R. Monroe wrote.

The incident that might have served to bring down the Reno Gang and went down in history books as the first train robbery began at about 6:30 p.m. on October 6, 1866. The Ohio & Mississippi train had just left the Seymour depot and was slowly winding its way east out of town when it was robbed by the Reno Gang. It was bad luck for the robbers, though, that a railroad agent happened to be aboard the train. The train company also happened to be under the protection of the Pinkerton Detective Agency.

Alerted to the robbery, the agent stopped the train not far from the crime scene, prompting the Reno Gang to abandon the big safe they had rolled from the train. Frustrated at not being able to pry open the safe with its reported $35,000 treasure and knowing the train agent and other men were on their trail, the Reno Gang made a quick getaway and left the safe behind.

A passenger on the train, George Kinney, identified two of the robbers as Renos. John and Simeon Reno were arrested, along with gang member Frank Sparks. But before the case went to trial, eyewitness Kinney was shot down in cold blood when he answered a late-night knock at his door.

Fed up with the murder and mayhem, Jackson County residents decided to take the law into their own hands. An estimated three hundred men formed a vigilante group known as the Scarlet Mask Society because of the long red bandanas they wore over their faces. Frank and John Reno thought it best to hightail it out of town to Missouri. On November 17, 1864, the Reno Gang robbed the Gallatin, Missouri, courthouse and got away with almost $24,000. One of the robbers was positively identified as John Reno.

When John Reno showed up back in Seymour on December 4, he was arrested and shipped back to Missouri to stand trial. On January 18, 1868, John Reno was sentenced to twenty-five years in Missouri State Penitentiary. Ironically, that might have saved his life.

With John Reno safely locked up, Frank Reno became the gang leader. Turning their attention to Iowa, the gang robbed and looted until Frank and other gang members were arrested in spring

1868. However, the jail couldn't hold them. Breaking a hole in the cell wall—and scrawling the message APRIL FOOLS above it—Frank Reno and the men escaped and headed back to Seymour for an even bigger heist.

On the night of May 22, 1868, the Reno Gang struck again. Less than twenty miles south of Seymour, they waylaid a train that was stopped at a refueling station. Uncoupling the engine and Adams Express car from the rest of the train, the robbers proceeded full speed ahead. They pistol whipped the railroad man in the express car and threw him out of the train. The man was found barely alive on the rail embankment the next morning.

With their haul of about $96,000, the Reno Gang stopped the train near Seymour, where the rest of the men waited with horses for the getaway. Although their leaders went into hiding, other gang members held up another train on July 10, 1868. But the unsuspecting men walked straight into a trap by the Pinkertons. Three of the bandits were captured and shipped by train to the county jail. They never made it.

Wearing red masks, a large vigilante mob stopped the train, grabbed the three robbers, and quickly strung them up from a nearby tree.

When three more gang members were captured, the Pinkertons decided to secretly take the prisoners by wagon instead of train for their legal day in court. But the vigilantes were not fooled. At the same place where their cohorts had met their hanging death, the three new prisoners were taken from the stopped wagon and lynched from the same beech tree. To this day, that spot is known as Hangman's Crossing.

As for the Renos, William and Simeon Reno were arrested at their Indianapolis hideout and taken to New Albany to await trial. Frank Reno and another gang member were arrested in Canada and transferred to New Albany. Law enforcement officials thought they had the Renos safe behind bars in a sturdy jail. But vigilantes had other ideas.

When almost one hundred vigilantes descended on the jail on December 12, 1868, law enforcement officers and other officials were no match for the angry lynch mob. Although the sheriff refused to hand over the cell keys, the vigilantes got what they wanted and went about their deadly business.

The vigilantes hung Frank Reno from an iron pillar near the stairwell on the second floor cellblock. With a noose around his neck, William Reno was quickly shoved over the landing next to his older brother. Putting up a mad fight, Simeon Reno was hanged in another corner of the jail. Gang member Charlie Anderson was also strung up.

Then the vigilantes were gone. Displayed in open-lidded pine coffins, the dead men were gawked at by thousands of citizens who paraded through the jail to witness that crime does not pay. The bodies of the three Reno brothers were then turned over to their family and buried in Seymour. John Reno got out of jail in 1878 and died at his home in Seymour in 1895.

DISCOVERY OF MARENGO CAVE

1883

Blanche Hiestand tucked some candles in her pocket, grabbed her younger brother Orris, and headed off to the local cemetery to search for a rumored cave. Working as a cook at a boarding school, Blanche had overheard a group of schoolboys talking about a hole they had found not far from the academy.

The boys planned a trip to see if the hole would lead to a big cave. But Blanche beat them to the discovery. Hurrying home after work, fifteen-year-old Blanche and her reluctant eleven-year-old brother slipped away before their parents noticed and found a deep sinkhole hidden in a grove of trees.

Cool air was streaming from the opening as Blanche crawled down into the small crevice. Quickly, Blanche was able to raise herself up on her hands and knees and yelled for her brother to join her. Blanche and Orris then carefully climbed down a steep slope of broken rock.

The rock was slick and water was dripping from numerous small openings in the ceiling. But soon the two were able to stand. Then they heard water falling from the ceiling and saw sparkling formations ahead in the darkness. Even in the dim candlelight, the beauty of the huge chamber was dazzling.

More than a century has passed since the two Indiana kids found Marengo Cave on September 6, 1883. And visitors have been flocking ever since to the U.S. National Landmark for a glimpse of one of the Midwest's finest natural wonders.

When Samuel Stewart, owner of the land, heard of the discovery, he gathered a group of men and boys from the town and led them into the cave. Recognizing the value of what had been found, Stewart immediately opened the cave for public viewing. About a week after Blanche and Orris found the cave, Stewart had a ticket booth on top of the cave; tours have been given at Marengo ever since. This early protection is largely responsible for the pristine condition found in most of the cave to this day.

During the year or so before the discovery of the cave, most of the virgin timber on the hillside surrounding the cave entrance was logged. Early geologists who visited the cavern theorized that the increased runoff from the hillsides into the sinkhole was a primary factor in opening a human-size hole in the bottom of the sink that the boys from the school must have stumbled upon.

According to current geologic theory, Marengo Cave began to form about one million years ago. There is no documented evidence that anyone ever entered the cave before its historic discovery by the Hiestand children.

The cave itself is about 5.2 miles in length and consists of drier upper-level passages and two parallel underground rivers. The park above the cavern covers 122 acres of forested hills and valleys.

The cavern was operated by the Stewart family and their heirs until 1955, when it was purchased by local businessman Floyd Denton, who had great plans for the cavern but died before the projects could be completed. The current owners, the Roberson family, purchased the cavern from Denton's heirs in 1973 and added camping, canoeing, additional tours, and horseback riding. They also greatly upgraded the facilities.

No matter what the outside weather, Marengo Cave has natural air-conditioning and heat. The temperature stays at 52°F year-round. Caves take on the rock layer temperature surrounding them. For example, in Florida and Texas, caves are about 70°F and clammy. In Indiana, caves have limestone, and the annual temperature of the Marengo area of southern Indiana is 52°F.

The cave has had a colorful and checkered history. It was an early destination of railroad excursions and the site of band concerts and many community functions, including dances. Church services as well as weddings have been held in the cave. Even during the depths of the Great Depression, the cave remained open because it was a tradition for many families to pay a visit. Several movies have been filmed in the cave, including *Madison* in 2001 and *Fire From Below* in 2009.

Marengo Cave has two tours. The Crystal Palace Tour is an easy forty-minute walk that winds its way through formation-filled rooms and past huge flowstone deposits. The tour is highlighted by a visit to the world-famous Crystal Palace, acknowledged by speleologists as one of the ten most beautiful cavern rooms anywhere.

The Dripstone Trail Tour takes an hour and ten minutes, covering a leisurely one-mile underground trail. First opened in 1979, the Dripstone Trail is known for its profusion of delicate soda straw formations and slender totem stalagmites.

Some of the dramatic formations include New York City (a jumble of totem stalagmites and columns), Falls of Fire, Indian Bacon, The Great Wall of China (a large rimstone dam), the Pipe Organ, the Elephant's Head, the Pillared Palace (a labyrinth of columns and flowstone masses), and Prison Bars. One of the most eye-catching spots is Mirror Lake. Though it is only inches deep, the lake looks like it would go down for miles and reflects perfectly the beautiful formations around it.

Marengo Cave also has sort of a reverse wishing well. Instead of tossing coins into a fountain, visitors to Marengo Cave for years have been flipping pennies at the ceiling.

Of course, one reason cave-goers do that is to see the coins stick above their heads. Instead of bouncing back down, the airborne pennies adhere to a half-inch-thick layer of soft clay clinging to the cave ceiling, which stays eternally moist due to the cave's 100 percent humidity. The result is a metallic ceiling, slowly turning blue-gray over the years.

Some generous visitors have tossed more than pennies at the ceiling. No one knows if they couldn't tell the difference between a penny and a nickel or a dime or a quarter in the dark or if they just felt like tossing larger change. The total included 5,750 quarters, 12,218 dimes, 11,806 nickels, and 60,596 pennies. The total weight of the money was nearly 500 pounds.

In addition, several hundred coins from foreign countries were taken off the ceiling. Most of the foreign money came from Canada, but other major foreign contributors were Germany, Britain, France, Japan, and Korea.

Once every decade or so the ceiling must be cleared of its coin cover. If not, the new coins wouldn't stand a chance of finding a muddy spot to stick. During its last cleaning, more than 90,000 coins, totaling $3,855.56, were collected. The money was donated to the Nature Conservancy, which is actively involved in protecting southern Indiana cave country and the Blue River.

But cleaning the ceiling is not an easy task. Workers must climb sixteen-foot ladders to reach directly above their heads and carefully pry coins from the mud. The money is then dropped into five-gallon plastic buckets. The coins must be gently pulled off by hand so as to not damage the ceiling.

The buckets of coins are dumped into a small concrete mixer, along with some mild vinegar. Bank machines can't be used to count the coins because the money is covered with dirt and grit. Even with cleaning, the coins could still jam sensitive bank counting equipment. Instead, the money is turned over to the Federal Reserve for redemption and will not be returned to circulation because of its corroded condition.

Over the years, curious people kept thinking there might be more to the cave than originally explored. Searchers first began digging back in the early 1900s. They'd dig for a while, then they'd give up. Then a new group would come along and dig some more.

All that work paid off on June 14, 1992, when some Marengo Cave employees made a breakthrough. The surprised workers found a 3.5-mile section of caves that holds the largest underground passage in the state of Indiana. The passage is so mammoth that several houses could easily fit in it. It looks as though it could easily hold a football stadium. As far as officials know, no one had ever been in there before.

That huge discovery is now open to brave hearts who don't mind crawling on their stomachs through dark, tight quarters and getting covered with mud. Crawlers are guaranteed to get wet and muddy.

Allowing for preparation and cleanup, the Waterfall Crawl at Marengo Cave takes about three hours and is available only by reservation. Explorers must be at least twelve years old and are provided with helmets and headlights. Explorers also are told to wear old clothes and old shoes and to bring clean clothes in a bag. When the crawl is over, participants immediately head to the showers for cleanup.

Waterfall Crawl starts in the Red Room, proceeds through Blowing Bat Crawl, the aptly named Pig Pen (about a fifty-foot belly crawl that is muddy like a pig pen), and on to the Valley of Lost Soles, filled with a soupy wet clay that can suck shoes off feet.

One of the highlights of Waterfall Crawl is a chance to see the Orris Hiestand Monument. It's a large cave formation that is directly located underneath Orris Hiestand's gravestone in the cemetery. He is buried right above the cave that he and his sister found.

DAN PATCH, THE GREATEST PACER HORSE OF THEM ALL

1896

When he was born, the mahogany-colored colt had legs so crooked that he couldn't stand. The newborn had to be helped to his feet so he could nurse. He was tall, scraggly, and clumsy, a great disappointment to his owner.

After all, the foal's father had been an outstanding pacer horse. But this bowlegged baby born on April 29, 1896, in Oxford, Indiana, didn't look like he would amount to much. Some folks even suggested that the colt with the crooked left hind leg be put out of his misery. At the most, they reasoned, he would probably end up hauling a delivery wagon. No way could he ever run with legs like that.

But Dan Patch went on to prove them all wrong. He grew up to become the most famous harness racing horse of all time. To this day, Dan Patch is a legend, a pacer who set world records and had adoring fans turn out for his every run.

Back then, the gangly colt was named after his owner—the "Dan" for local storekeeper Daniel Messner Jr.—and his sire—the

"Patch" for racehorse Joe Patchen. Seeing no future for the colt, Messner originally tried to trade him for another horse owned by local livery stable owner John Wattles. Since Wattles wouldn't agree to the deal, Messner offered to pay him to train the colt. By the time he was four years old, Dan Patch had grown into a beautiful horse. He stood sixteen hands tall or sixty-four inches and weighed a good 1,165 pounds. A white star gleamed in the center of his forehead, perhaps a foretelling of his future.

Dan Patch was friendly, intelligent, and eager to please. But the big question remained: Could he run?

At four years old, Dan Patch showed naysayers exactly what he could do.

On August 30, 1900, in Boswell, Indiana, Dan Patch easily outpaced his competitors and was a beauty to watch. In harness racing, the jockey doesn't ride on the horse's back. Instead, the jockey rides in a lightweight two-wheeled, single-seat cart pulled by the horse. Known as Standardbreds, horses in this race form are divided into either pacers or trotters. A trotter moves its legs diagonally, right front and left hind, then left front and right hind, hitting the ground at the same time. As a pacer, Dan Patch moved his legs laterally, right front and right hind, then left front and left hind, striking the ground simultaneously.

When he raced, Dan Patch had a custom cart to keep his crazy legs from hitting the wheels and custom-made shoes to balance his stride. He ran as though he didn't know there was anything wrong with his legs.

Turn-of-the-century pacer races were conducted in heats—usually five one-mile contests. Riders would warm up their horses for a few miles, then launch into the heats until one horse won the majority, usually three heats out of the five. In his long career, Dan Patch never lost a race.

About this time, M.E. Sturgis of Buffalo, New York, offered Messner the unheard-of sum of $20,000 for Dan Patch. After the poisoning death of another of his horses, Messner was said to have worried about the safety of Dan Patch. Messner took the money and the horse had a new home. But by July of 1902, Dan Patch had become such a winner that there was no owner who wanted to match his horse against the pacer. It was a foregone conclusion that Dan Patch would wipe out every competitor in sight.

With the public clamoring to see the horse run, Sturgis did the only thing he could do—he had Dan Patch race against time. In exhibition trials, Dan Patch would run against the clock. At the 1906 Minnesota State Fair on September 8, Dan Patch electrified the racing world by pacing a mile in one minute, fifty-five seconds, a world record. Although unofficial, the record was accepted and the charismatic Dan Patch was at the top of his game.

Not only was he a champ at pacing, but Dan Patch also won the hearts of the public. He loved children and would let them run under his belly while he stood still. Before an exhibition, Dan Patch would cast his eyes over the crowd as if to say, "So, you came to see me. Well, I'm going to give you a show you'll enjoy." After a race, he would stop in front of the grandstand and bow to the crowd. Onlookers went wild.

In December 1902, Dan Patch was sold again for a whopping $60,000 to Marion Willis Savage of Minneapolis. Owner of the International Stock Food Company, Savage knew he had a major marketing treasure in Dan Patch. Savage lavished luxuries on his horse and showed him off to the world. Dan Patch now lived in a palatial palace nicknamed the "Taj Mahal," complete with running water, steam heat, a state-of-the art outdoor mile track, and an enclosed, heated half-mile track. Dan traveled in his own railroad car, which boasted his likeness on either side.

With a flair for showmanship, Savage promoted his famed horse to become one of the most successfully merchandised sports figures in history. Dan Patch's name and likeness were used to endorse everything from washing machines and china to chewing tobacco and manure spreaders. Admirers could buy silver-plated Dan Patch horseshoes, stop watches, thermometers, hobbyhorses, and sleds. Folks danced the Dan Patch Two Step to the song of the same name. There was even a Dan Patch automobile that sold for $525.

In 1909 Dan Patch was racing at an exhibition in Los Angeles when he began visibly limping. He was forced to retire and returned to the stables where devoted fans from around the nation came to visit him.

When he died in 1916, Dan Patch again made headlines, as did his owner. Both Dan and Savage fell sick on the Fourth of July. Hospitalized, Savage was recovering from minor surgery. Dan Patch appeared better, too. Then Dan Patch took a turn for the worse. The magnificent horse died July 11 of an enlarged heart at twenty years old, his hooves flailing the air in one last dash down the home stretch.

Hearing that his beloved pacer was gone, Savage died the following day. The devoted master is said to have died of a broken heart over the loss of his cherished Dan Patch.

THE FIRST INDY 500

1911

The rumble of snarling engines mingled with the thunderous roar of more than 80,000 people at Indianapolis Motor Speedway. Resplendent in a spiffy white suit, Carl Fisher drove the pace car, a Stoddard-Dayton roadster, to lead the pack of forty race cars in the first of what would become a Memorial Day tradition.

Amid a haze of heavy smoke from burning fuel and oil, Fisher proudly motored along at forty miles an hour, then veered to the left near the starting line. From the trackside, Fred "Pop" Wagner waved his red flag, and the first Indy 500 run on Tuesday, May 30, 1911, was on its way into racing history.

And it all started with a crazy idea.

In the early part of the twentieth century, Indiana was the second largest manufacturer of automobiles in America. Hoosier cars tended to be more expensive and of better quality than those made in Michigan, but all vehicles then could have used a higher testing standard. In 1905 Indianapolis auto parts manufacturer Carl Fisher was helping racing friends in France when he observed that Europeans had an edge over the American automobile industry. What his country needed, Fisher decided, was a good way of testing cars before putting them on the road.

At the time, American racing was just getting a foothold on horse tracks and even on public roads. But a good automobile racetrack would go a long way, Fisher reasoned. He pitched the idea to three friends and fellow businessmen: James Allison, Arthur Newby, and Frank Wheeler.

Together the four men bought a 328-acre plot of land northwest of downtown Indianapolis for $72,000. But the first race at the new speedway wasn't vehicles. It was balloons. Though the track wasn't completed, on the evening of June 5, 1909, nine gas-filled balloons lifted off at the newly christened Indianapolis Motor Speedway, racing for bragging rights and silver trophies. The winner of the Speedway's first competitive event, *University City*, landed 382 miles away in Alabama after spending more than a day aloft.

Surfaced with a combination of crushed stone and asphalt, the track opened for its first auto race on August 19, 1909. Paying $1 for one of the grandstand seats or 50 cents for the first- and second-turn bleachers, between 15,000 and 20,000 spectators came for the big event. Impatient drivers didn't wait for the official start, and flag-man Pop Wagner had to stop the field three times and finally begin it from a standing start.

The race was a treacherous, dangerous one. The track's surface broke up from the heat and the traffic, resulting in the deaths of two drivers, two mechanics, and two spectators. Louis Schwitzer won the first race of the day in his Stoddard-Dayton. But the disaster pointed out the necessity of repaving the track. This time they used street-paving bricks— 3,200,000 of them in fact. The job took sixty-three days. By the time the project was finished, the track had already been nicknamed "The Brickyard."

The new brick surface did the job, and the first official race on the new track took place on December 17, 1909. However, fans didn't continue to pack the stands. To draw the public, Fisher and his partners decided they needed something bigger, something unheard of, a really spectacular one-day annual event instead of a series of minor races. That's how the Indy 500 was born.

The inaugural Indianapolis 500-Mile Race was announced for Memorial Day 1911. Making it five hundred miles was a big deal, meaning the race would last almost a workday between mid-morning and late afternoon. With the speed of cars in those days, it would take about seven hours for racers to run five hundred miles. Fisher figured seven hours would be the right amount of time for fans to be at the Speedway and watch the race.

The race generated big interest from the beginning. So many people descended on the city that hotels didn't have enough rooms and restaurants ran out of food. "Never before in its history has the city entertained a larger throng," reported *The Indianapolis News*.

With so many people arriving at once, downtown streets were gridlocked. On dawn of the big day, fifteen special trains unloaded thousands of people from such big cities as Chicago, St. Louis, and Cincinnati. The Speedway scene was sheer bedlam. All 33,000 reserved seats were sold out at $1.50 a piece. General admission tickets at $1 were also gone. Crowds lined both sides of the field fencing along the track. Others bought special tickets that allowed them to watch the race from their parked cars. Some estimates placed the crowd at almost 100,000.

And spectators weren't disappointed. With a huge winning purse of $27,500, forty-six groups had filled out entry forms, and forty-four racers showed up. One had an accident and couldn't race, one car broke down, and two others didn't qualify because they were too slow. On the big day, it was forty race cars set to go with positions decided by the order in which the entry was received in the mail.

To put himself in the spotlight, as well as to let spectators get a better look at the competitors, Fisher decided to lead the cars around the track in a parade lap. Since he was a Stoddard-Dayton dealer, the consummate showman decided to take that lap in a Stoddard-Dayton. It was the first known rolling start of a major auto race and the first use of a pace car.

Among the race favorites was Ray Harroun who had come out of retirement to run the first 500. His vehicle was a yellow and black No. 32 Marmon Wasp, which he had designed. Driving the only single-seat car in the race, Harroun didn't have room for a ride-along mechanic as did the other cars to keep an eye on oil levels and watch for danger. Because he didn't have a mechanic to warn of other cars passing, Harroun devised a four-posted rearview mirror. Some say that was the first known rearview mirror on an automobile. Ironically, Harroun later said that the mirror vibrated so much that he couldn't see out of it anyway.

Another favored driver was Ralph Mulford. His racer was a Lozier passenger car he had driven down from Detroit. With its headlights and fenders removed, the Lozier was faster but ended up needing more pit stops to replace worn tires. When the race was over, Mulford drove his Lozier back to Chicago, replaced the headlights and fenders, and sold it as a used car.

Spectators were mesmerized from the get-go. Of the forty starters, only twelve actually ran the full two hundred laps. Despite dire predictions of automotive mayhem, only one fatality occurred. Sam Dickson, a mechanic riding with Arthur Greiner, was killed when Greiner's car hit the wall in the southeast turn.

Avoiding the pileups, the local guy—Harroun in his Wasp— crossed the finish line with a time of six hours, forty-two minutes, and eight seconds. He covered five hundred miles with an average speed of 74.59 miles per hour. Harroun was proclaimed the winner of the first Indy 500.

But there are those, including pioneer race car driver Ralph Mulford, who claim another man actually won that first race. On the thirteenth lap, a multicar accident on the main straightaway in front of the scoring stand sent the scorers (many of them untrained, just Fisher's friends) scurrying. For several laps, no one was scoring the race. That's when Mulford claimed he wasn't credited with a lap he completed—a lap that would have made him the winner. Mulford went to his grave contending he had been the first 500 winner.

While officials wrestled all night with the scoring controversy, Fisher was ecstatic about his inaugural Indy 500. As he celebrated, Fisher began to plan an even bigger spectacle for the next Memorial Day. However, not everyone wanted to see such chaos again. An editorial the next day in *The Indianapolis News* proclaimed that "interesting and thrilling as was the race at the speedway yesterday, it is to be hoped that we have seen the last of these 500-mile contests."

Of course, that wasn't the end of the Indy 500. In 1957 the 500 Festival began to organize community activities to celebrate "The Greatest Spectacle in Racing." The 500 Festival Parade became a major event, drawing thousands of people to downtown Indianapolis. Today, the 500 Festival is a monthlong celebration of events honoring the Indy 500. Highlights include the country's largest half-marathon, downtown parade, memorial celebrations for the nation's servicemen and women, Kid's Day festivities, and Community Day at the Indianapolis Motor Speedway.

Gentlemen (and ladies) start their engines at the Indianapolis Motor Speedway long before race day. Throughout May, hordes of racing fans knock off work and head to the track for qualifications, when drivers vie for the thirty-three coveted positions of the India-napolis 500. Crowds are thickest on Pole Day, the first round of qualifications; Bump Day, the final chance for racers to make the starting grid; and Carb Day, the last practice before race day, fol-lowed by a free rock concert.

FIRST TRANSCONTINENTAL RADIO BROADCAST OF A FUNERAL

1931

Clustered near radios, listeners around the world heard the words emanating from South Bend, Indiana, on April 5, 1931. For the first time in the history of broadcasting, a funeral was covered by an international radio hookup.

Broadcast live coast to coast on CBS Radio and sent by shortwave to Europe, South America, and Asia, the service marked a world coming together in grief at the death of one man.

"Knute Rockne is dead," Charles O'Donnell, president of the University of Notre Dame, began his eulogy at the funeral. "And who was he?"

President Herbert Hoover mourned Rockne's passing in a plane crash as "a national loss." The king of Norway sent a special delegation to the funeral. State legislators passed resolutions of sympathy and condolences. Newspapers ran editorials in his memory.

"Ask men and women from every walk of life, ask the children, ask the boys of America. Ask any and all of these, who was this man whose death has struck the nation with dismay and has everywhere bowed heads in grief," O'Donnell said.

How could a college football coach have inspired such devotion that his death at age forty-three would bring about such unprecedented press coverage?

"You died a national hero … Notre Dame was your address, but every gridiron in America was your home," said popular syndicated columnist Will Rogers, who, ironically enough, would die in an air crash himself in Alaska just four years later.

At the end of the 1930 football season, Rockne was on his way to Los Angeles aboard a Transcontinental-Western flight from Kansas City. The plane encountered a storm shortly after takeoff and crashed in a rural area near Bazaar, Kansas. All eight onboard were killed. Legend says that the passengers and crew were aware of their fate. When Rockne's body was recovered by a rescue crew, it was said the coach had a rosary clutched in his hand.

The Knute Rockne story started on March 4, 1888, when he was born in Voss, Norway. When Knute was five, his father, a carriage maker, moved the family to Chicago. Neighborhood youngsters would spend long evenings playing sandlot baseball and football, American games that were unheard of in Norway.

Following his father's musical lead (Lars was a skilled cornet player), Knute began playing the flute. It was a passion he enjoyed for the rest of his life. Football, however, was not something his parents wanted their small son to be playing. Afraid he would be severely injured in the rough sport, his parents forbade him to play. Knute, of course, slipped away to the neighborhood football field whenever he could. A short, scrawny kid, Knute took more than his share of injuries.

At Chicago's North West Division High School, Rockne ran track and played football for a short time. Dropping out of school,

Rockne had a series of odd jobs and at age nineteen got a job as a postal clerk. When he heard that a couple of his buddies were headed to Notre Dame, Rockne decided to give it a try. Although he knew nothing about Notre Dame, Rockne quickly discovered that the university had a football team and that scored it for him. After passing an entrance exam, the twenty-two-year-old Rockne enrolled at Notre Dame in 1910.

Still seeking its place in the sun, Notre Dame was a small college surrounded by farms and gently rolling Hoosier countryside. Rockne wasn't built like a powerhouse football player, but he made it on the team and played fullback and end. When the 1911 season started, Notre Dame had a new head coach—Jack Marks, formerly of Dartmouth. Under Marks, Notre Dame began experimenting with the forward pass.

More or less a haphazard move, the forward pass was a thing of beauty under Rockne and quarterback Gus Dorais. When the two got summer jobs at Cedar Point in Ohio, they took along a football and spent much of their free time practicing forward passes on the beach.

Spectators were not used to seeing a football thrown in the air. After all, footballs were made for kicking. But Rockne and Dorais made throwing and receiving a football into an art form. When the 1913 Notre Dame team suited up with Rockne as captain under new coach Jess Harper, they were ready to make gridiron history.

Only a small crowed turned out for the Army versus Notre Dame game. It was a foregone conclusion that the mighty Army would win. Notre Dame was just a blip on the Army game schedule. Imagine the amazement when Notre Dame defeated Army 35–13. Dorais and Rockne completed a great majority of forward passes for that score.

Graduating with honors and a bachelor's degree in chemistry and pharmacology in 1914, Rockne considered going to medical school in St. Louis. But he decided to stay at Notre Dame to teach chemistry and be a football assistant. In Rockne's four years as assistant, Notre Dame lost only five games. Offered the head coaching job at Michigan State, Rockne turned it down and took over as head coach at Notre Dame in 1918 when Harper resigned.

Rockne's record as a coach is one of the most remarkable that any coach of any sport has ever compiled. His 1918 and 1919 teams went unbeaten. Perhaps his greatest teams were in 1920, 1924, 1929, and 1930. And the most memorable player was certainly a young man named George Gipp

Called by Rockne the "greatest player Notre Dame ever produced," Gipp was a magnificent athlete. At Notre Dame on a baseball scholarship, Gipp caught Rockne's attention and joined the Fighting Irish; he would eventually be nominated as the first Notre Dame player in history to make the All-America first team. But Gipp seemed to have contacted a throat infection that just wouldn't go away. A few weeks after the close of the 1920 season, "the Gipper" was dying with Rockne by his bedside.

As lore has it, these were the words that Gipp spoke from his deathbed on December 14, 1920:

> *"I've got to go, Rock. It's all right. I'm not afraid.*
> *Sometime, Rock, when the team is up against it, when*
> *things are wrong and the breaks are beating the boys—*
> *tell them to go in there with all they've got and win*
> *just one for the Gipper. I don't know where I'll be*
> *then, Rock. But I'll know about it, and I'll be happy."*

As Gipp requested, those words were used to inspire the team in a game against Army in 1928. And they did "win one for the Gipper." During thirteen years as head coach, Rockne's teams compiled 105 victories, twelve losses, five ties, and six national championships with five undefeated seasons.

Rockne was a winner off the field as well. He was considered an inspiring father figure to his players and was a major force in the development of a whole batch of top-notch coaches. Rockne preached hard work to everyone around him. "The best thing I ever learned in life was that things have to be worked for," Rockne once said.

Not surprisingly, Hollywood came calling. Troubled by phlebitis, Rockne was advised by his doctors to take it easy. But he headed off to meet with moviemakers anyway. On March 31, 1931, Rockne boarded a plane with five fellow passengers and two pilots at the Kansas City airport to fly to California. A light snow was falling as the plane took off shortly after 9:00 a.m. In eastern Kansas, the plane became enveloped in a thick fog. Near the tiny town of Bazaar, some ranchers working with their cattle saw the plane emerging from a big cloud nearly 90 degrees off course. Suddenly, the plane lost part of its left wing and plunged toward the snow-covered prairie. No one survived the violent wreck. Most of the bodies were crushed beyond recognition.

On the day of the funeral, April 4, flags flew at half-mast and businesses shut down in South Bend. People around the world listened to the service broadcast live on the radio.

Rockne was laid to rest two miles from the Notre Dame campus in Highland Cemetery. His grave lies near an ancient tree named Council Oak where Native Americans once held council.

Almost a decade later, the Hollywood film for which Rockne had taken his last flight was released. *Knute Rockne: All-American* starred Pat O'Brien as Rockne and future president Ronald Reagan as George Gipp.

More than half a century after his death, Rockne became the first coach in any sport to be honored with a commemorative stamp. The day the stamp was issued, March 9, 1988, President Reagan delivered a speech at Notre Dame before a capacity crowd of 10,000, many of whom hadn't even been born when Knute Rockne died.

JOHN DILLINGER ESCAPES FROM JAIL

1934

Bold headlines shouted the news: John Dillinger had escaped from jail.

Carving a fake gun from a block of wood and staining it with black shoe polish, Dillinger had broken out of the so-called escape proof jail in Crown Point, Indiana, on March 3, 1934. Adding insult to injury, Dillinger made his getaway in the sheriff's new V-8 Ford.

The FBI's first "public enemy" was on the loose again. But he wouldn't be free for long. Before the year had ended, the thirty-one-year-old Hoosier gangster would be dead.

Born June 22, 1903, in the Oak Hill section of Indianapolis, John Herbert Dillinger Jr. grew up in a middle-class home. His father was a grocer who tried to steer his son on the straight and narrow path, believing in "spare the rod and spoil the child." Dillinger's mother died shortly before his fourth birthday. When his father remarried seven years later, Dillinger is said to have resented his stepmother but later grew to love her.

Frequently in trouble with the law for fighting and petty theft, Dillinger quit school at age sixteen and went to work in an Indianapolis plywood mill. Fearing that the big city was corrupting his son, Dillinger's father moved the family to a farm in the tiny town of Mooresville. Dillinger didn't take the move kindly. Small-town life was boring to him.

Besides getting in trouble, his main interests were hunting, baseball, and girls. He excelled at all three. Hoping to escape his problems, Dillinger enlisted in the Navy, was shipped off to the Great Lakes Training Center, and completed basic training on October 4, 1923. Assigned to the battleship *Utah* as a fireman, Dillinger soon grew tired of shoveling coal into the ship's boilers and went AWOL. Eventually dishonorably discharged from the Navy, Dillinger returned home, where he met and married Beryl Hovious on April 12, 1924.

Unable to hold a job, Dillinger and an older man named Ed Singleton hatched a plan to rob a local grocer. The plan went awry and the two men were arrested the next day. Singleton got an attorney, pleaded not guilty, and was sentenced to two to fifteen years. Following the advice of his father, Dillinger confessed to the crime and was sentenced to ten to twenty years in prison. Both father and son were shocked.

Enraged at the system and at his father, Dillinger headed off to prison, vowing, "I'll be the meanest bastard you ever saw when I get out." In prison, Dillinger had plenty of time and hardened cohorts to learn how to be a more successful criminal. Later transferred to Indiana State Penitentiary, Dillinger was now with the worst of the worst. "I went in a carefree boy," he wrote his father. "I came out bitter toward everything."

Paroled on May 10, 1933, mostly at the strong behest of his father and family, after serving eight and a half years, Dillinger left prison an angry young man. His wife had divorced him while he was incarcerated, but Dillinger had made new friends—Harry "Pete" Pierpoint, Charles Makley, Homer Van Meter, and Russell Clark— who would later become his gang members.

With the nation deep in the Great Depression, Dillinger turned to his former trade. Almost immediately he robbed a bank in Bluffton, Ohio, and was arrested on September 22. Frisking him, county jailers found what looked like the plan for a prison break. Dillinger denied any such plan, but four days later, eight of his friends escaped from the Indiana State Prison using the same plan. Heading to the Lima jail, three of the escapees freed Dillinger by claiming they were transferring him to the very same jail they had just managed to escape.

From then on, it was a crime spree—robbing banks and police arsenals. For some, Dillinger became a hero of sorts. Many people had lost their savings when banks failed during the Great Depression, and they cheered on the likeable robber. On December 12, a Dillinger gang member shot and killed a police detective in Chicago. A month later, the Dillinger gang killed a police officer during a robbery of the First National Bank of East Chicago in Indiana.

Hiding out in Florida and later in Tucson, Arizona, gang members were caught when a fire broke out in their hotel room. Registered under assumed names, Clark and Makley were identified by firemen and arrested, as were Dillinger and Pierpoint.

Newsreel footage showed Dillinger arriving in Crown Point to await trial and execution. When the heavily guarded Dillinger landed at Midway Airport in Chicago after his arrest on January 30, 1934, several thousand people turned out to get a glimpse of him. "This is the end of Dillinger," Lake County Prosecutor Robert Estill announced, not knowing that the city's law enforcement would soon become a national joke.

Armed deputies stood atop the jail and other deputies sur-rounded the car when the handcuffed Dillinger was escorted into the jail. Sheriff Lillian Holley, who had taken over the job just months before when her sheriff husband was killed, swore that Dillinger would not escape from her jail.

When officials allowed journalists access to their prisoner, Dill-inger denied being in East Chicago or killing a police officer. Spread in newspapers across America, a photograph showed prosecutor Estill and Sheriff Holley smiling proudly and posing with their prisoner. The photo was shockingly chummy, with Dillinger resting his elbow on the shoulder of the prosecutor while Estill has his arm around the alleged murderer.

With the gang safely behind bars, the legal system began its slow paperwork grind to send Dillinger to the electric chair. The trial was set for March 12. But Dillinger didn't wait that long.

Early on the morning of Saturday, March 3, 1934—five weeks after his celebrity arrival at the Crown Point jail—Dill-inger made his move. Sticking the wooden gun in a guard's back, Dillinger ordered him to open the door to his cell. Locking up more guards and several trusties, Dillinger armed himself and invited another inmate, Herbert Youngblood, to go with him. Youngblood had little to lose. The black man was already in for murder and facing execution. He would die in a gun battle several months later. All in all, the two men locked up more than two dozen prison personnel.

With Deputy Sheriff Ernest Blunk as hostage, the two escapees helped themselves to weapons and walked across the street to the city garage, where they took mechanic Edward Saager hostage and climbed in the fastest car available: Sheriff Holley's personal Ford. Once the escapees were safely on the road, they let Blunk and Saager out, giving them money for fare back home.

That night, the sheriff's car was found abandoned in Chicago. The embarrassed sheriff said the breakout was "too ridiculous for words" and vowed that she would lead the search for Dillinger and personally shoot him herself. Although Dillinger later told his father that he had used a safety razor blade to slowly carve the fake gun out of the top brace off a washboard, reports still linger that corrupt police officers and maybe even Dillinger's own attorney helped the convict to escape.

When Dillinger was at large, sightings began almost immediately. And it was obvious that even the escape artist couldn't be in all those places at the same time. Outraged at the escape, the FBI organized a nationwide manhunt. Still, Dillinger made one last visit home on April 8 for a family reunion. Some said it was to tell his father and family goodbye. Family photos recall that time, including a famous one of a snappily dressed Dillinger smiling in the family's farmyard, his machine gun in one hand and his wooden pistol in the other.

By April 23, 1934, the Dillinger Gang was hiding out in Little Bohemia Lodge in Wisconsin. Tipped off to their whereabouts by the lodge owners, federal agents surrounded the place and opened fire, killing one Civilian Conservation Corps worker and injuring two more innocents. Dillinger and his men leaped from a second-story window into a deep snowbank behind the building and made their getaway.

Frustrated at the Little Bohemia fiasco, FBI leader J. Edgar Hoover and agent Melvin Purvis were red-faced at their failure. Dillinger seemed to have dropped out of sight. Then the feds got a huge tip. Afraid of being deported to her native Romania and hoping to pocket reward money, a Chicago prostitute named Anna Sage said she could lead the men to Dillinger. During a heat wave in Chicago,

Dillinger, his girlfriend Polly Hamilton, and Anna Sage were going to the Biograph Theatre to cool off on the night of July 22.

Determined not to kill any more innocent bystanders, the feds set up several codes to be sure it was Dillinger. To alert the FBI, Anna Sage would wear an orange skirt that would look red under the marquee lights. Purvis would wait outside the theater, lighting a cigar to signal that Dillinger was on his way.

The movie that Sunday was a crime thriller, *Manhattan Melodrama,* starring Clark Gable. The movie ended with the hero walking a last mile to the electric chair. Moments later, wearing a straw hat and gold-rimmed eyeglasses, Dillinger walked a few yards to an ambush death in a nearby alley. Leaving the theater with his girlfriend on one arm and Anna Sage on the other at about 10:30 p.m., Dillinger suddenly sensed that something was terribly wrong. Seeing an alley as the nearest escape route, Dillinger turned the girls loose, crouched, and started to run, reaching for the .380 automatic pistol in his right pocket.

He never made it. Brought down in a hail of bullets from almost thirty feds, Dillinger crumbled to the sidewalk. Pandemonium erupted. Two women who were standing nearby had been injured by G-men gunfire. There were reports of men dipping their handkerchiefs and women the hems of their skirts into the pools of Dillinger's blood as souvenirs of that fateful day.

In his pocket, one of the nation's most successful bank robbers had $7.70. The public was so enthralled with Dillinger that his body was put on display in the Cook County morgue where 15,000 people filed through for a grisly glimpse.

In Mooresville, Dillinger's father told the press, "I suspect that Johnnie would rather it had been that way. He never told me so, but they had laid so many things on him that I guess he would rather have been shot down than arrested again."

Dillinger's casket was lowered into the ground at Crown Hill Cemetery in Indianapolis during a summer rainstorm three days after his death. He was buried next to his mother. About five thousand people attended the funeral, some ravaging the site after the burial, stealing flowers and even scoops of mud. Fearing that vandals might dig up his son's body, Dillinger's father later had his son's coffin reburied under a thick layer of concrete and scrap iron. Dillinger's tombstone has had to be replaced several times because of vandalism by people chipping off pieces as keepsakes.

HAUNTED WILLARD LIBRARY

1937

On a cold, snowy night, the janitor at the Willard Library in Evansville was making his usual rounds. It was his chore to shovel coal into the furnace at 3:00 a.m.

As he entered the dark basement, the janitor nearly bumped into a shadowy figure. Focusing his flashlight, the janitor froze at the ghostly sight of a veiled lady dressed in glowing grey. Even her shoes were grey.

That was in 1937. It was recorded as the first known sighting of "The Grey Lady." After that, the janitor quit.

Since then, countless employees and patrons have reported seeing the apparition. So popular has she become that ghost tours are offered around Halloween each year, and a ghost cam of various rooms in the library invites people to look for her at any time of the year.

Funded by Evansville philanthropist Willard Carpenter, the Victorian Gothic structure was opened in 1885 in what is now the oldest public library building in Indiana. Listed on the National

Register of Historic Places, Willard Library was the dream of a man who received very little formal education but was said to be very intelligent and successful.

One of twelve children in a Vermont farming family, Carpenter left home at the age of eighteen with $7 in his pocket. Known as the "born king of real estate speculators," Carpenter became one of the most powerful and influential Democrats in Evansville and served as a city councilman for thirty years.

On August 23, 1876, Willard and his wife, Lucina, executed a deed of trust, conveying property for the library. Lucina reportedly opposed the idea but didn't have much chance against her strong-willed husband. With construction in full swing by 1883, eighty-year-old Willard Carpenter was on the job site every day, inspecting the work of the paid laborers and working himself. Not everyone was delighted that the wealthy Carpenter was hauling around wheelbarrows and climbing up on the roof. His family was said to be highly embarrassed, and workmen were known to grumble about having Carpenter's watchful eyes on them daily.

That came to an end around Halloween 1883 when Carpenter suffered a paralyzing stroke. On November 3, he died.

Carpenter's monument to himself was completed the following year at a cost of nearly $60,000. After it was furnished and stocked with almost ten thousand books, Willard Library was ready for a grand opening on March 28, 1885. And it was a real beauty. With a wide stone stairway leading into the vestibule with its unique patterned tile flooring, the library features heavy oak finished woodwork and corniced ceilings. With plate glass and ornamental stained-glass windows, the library has lovely furnishings and beautifully carved wood staircases. The library is renowned for its Thrall Art Book Collection, which includes rare and valuable volumes and magazines. A popular community landmark, Willard Library is known for its programs, extensive collection, and huge wealth of genealogical records, including photographs, newspapers, and city directories dating back to the 1840s.

But it is the lady in grey that prompts the most discussion and speculation.

No one is afraid of her. But many people have had strange things happen to them at the library. The list is long:

Footsteps when no one is around. The strong smell of heavy perfume from a mysterious source. An empty elevator that goes up and down, with floor buttons lighting and doors opening. Bathroom faucets turned on forcefully by unseen hands. Motion sensor devices set off when the library is closed and vacant. Unseen hands touching a visitor's hair or earrings.

Books that fall off shelves. A chair that is repeatedly pulled out after it is pushed in. A file box jumping off a desk and spilling its contents in a fan shape. A photograph of a woman standing in a library window that is blocked and inaccessible. A feeling of cold when there should be none.

A second janitor also had an encounter with the Grey Lady in the early hours of the morning when he bumped into her in the basement. After numerous other encounters, he quit, too.

During a visit to the library, lecturers from the University of Southern Indiana say they saw the ghost. Policemen responding to a security alarm at the library spotted two ghosts in an upstairs window of the library.

And similar experiences have happened to people of all ages.

Back in the 1960s, some small children were raising quite a ruckus at a library party, running and skipping on the hallway stairs. Suddenly, a little three-year-old ran to his mother, afraid of a woman who was reprimanding them. The little boy said she was a ghost lady shaking her finger at him. The party ended rather abruptly.

Longtime librarian Margaret Maier felt the hauntings were most strong when the library was being disrupted by construction. Maier believed the Grey Lady went home with her in 1874 when library renovations were going on. On the way home that day, Maier complained of her automobile being inexplicably cold. She also woke up cold the next morning at home.

Maier and her sister Ruth felt an unseen presence was in their home. The two sisters also noted in their home the strong smell of heavy perfume.

Countless speculation and opinions exist about whose ghost the famed Grey Lady actually is. Some believe the ghost traveled from a nearby cemetery. The Discovery Channel, ghost hunters, and psychics have visited Willard Library trying to determine who the spectral image might be.

Since the Grey Lady likes to hang out in the children's room, some say she lost a child and is waiting for the child to come back. Others say that a woman died in the building during its early days and that she liked the library so much she never left and gets jealous when mortals read her treasured books.

Still others believe the lady in grey is actually the ghost of Louise Carpenter, daughter of the library's founder. Louise was bitter that her father gave money for the library. Upon Willard's death, Louise thought she would inherit a large fortune. Instead, she received nothing and the library inherited a handsome amount. She sued the library's Board of Trustees, trying to stop the library, claiming that her father was "of unsound mind and was unduly influenced in establishing (Willard) Library."

She lost the suit and, as a result, her claim to any of the library's property. After her death, the story goes, Louise's spirit returned to the place that caused her so much grief during her life—Willard Library.

Those who subscribe to this opinion say that Louise will continue to haunt the library until the property and its holdings are turned back over to the living heirs of the Willard Carpenter family.

Others disagree with this theory because the ghost's dress is of an earlier period than the 1890s. Well-known parapsychologist Lucille Warren conducted an investigation in 1985. After seeing the spirit in the Children's Room, Warren said that the ghost did not intend to harm anyone and, indeed, did not even know she was haunting a library. The woman possibly committed suicide by drowning in a nearby canal and was haunting the property upon which the library was built.

Since Willard Library has installed several web cams and created a popular Web site, people often tune in to the site, hoping to catch a glimpse of the Grey Lady and to record their findings.

COLUMBUS ARCHITECTURAL
BIRTH STARTS

1942

Walk out a church designed by Eliel Saarinen, cross the street past a Henry Moore sculpture, and enter a library designed by I.M. Pei.

Where else in the world are such architectural treasures gathered in such a relatively small place? Like the famed explorer for which the city is named, Columbus, Indiana, has dared to reach great heights in its architectural quest.

No small town—and few big cities—in America can match Columbus for its modern architecture, which has earned praise across the nation. *Smithsonian Magazine* called Columbus a "veritable museum of modern architecture." Another admirer, Lady Bird Johnson, noted that "it is said that architecture is frozen music, but seldom in history has a group of artists produced such a symphony in stone as presents itself to the eye in Columbus."

The American Institute of Architects includes Columbus on its top six list, of cities for best architectural innovation and design right behind Chicago, New York, San Francisco, Boston, and Washington

D.C. Architectural marvels are scattered throughout the town, more than sixty buildings designed by some of the world's great architects. Local lore says that the county jail in Columbus looks so good that a visitor once tried to check in.

Surrounded by flat cornfields, Columbus (population 39,059) began its unlikely love affair with architecture in 1942 when its First Christian Church needed a new building for a growing congregation. Organized in 1855, the church was meeting in a brick Gothic building that was built in 1878. Two members of the congregation, William G. Irwin and his sister, Linnie Sweeney, wife of the minister Reverend Z. T. Sweeney, gave the church a parcel of land on Fifth Street for a new building.

In a daring move, the church selected a modern architect, Eliel Saarinen, to design the new church. He suggested breaking away from traditional Gothic and Georgian styles and creating a contemporary building. "The last drop of expressiveness has been squeezed out of these once so expressive styles," Saarinen said.

Completed in 1942, the First Christian Church broke with tradition and was the first modern-style church in America. Occupying a full city block, the church features simple, clean lines and no stained glass. Instead of a steeple, the church has a freestanding 166-foot bell tower adorned with a grid of translucent plastic panels. Constructed mostly of buff brick and limestone, the church has a geometric design with a large stone cross above the main entrance. Inside, deep-set windows running the full height of the walls direct light into the chancel.

Inside the sanctuary, a wall of wood is accented with masses of growing hoya. A double wooden gateway opens to reveal the baptistry pool. On the west wall hangs a tapestry of "The Sermon on the Mount," designed by Eliel Saarinen and his wife, Loja.

As Columbus grew in the years following World War II, new schools became necessary for the baby boom. Also the late J. Erwin Miller, chief executive officer of the Cummins Engine Company until his retirement in 1977, wanted to improve the quality of life in his hometown so he could stay there and convince others to relocate to the small Midwestern site. To attract the brain trust and top-quality workers that Cummins needed, Miller came up with a plan to emphasize art and architecture. His plan created a ripple effect that spread throughout the community.

Miller was a strong believer in Winston Churchill's statement: "First we shape our buildings, then our buildings shape us." When Miller died on August 16, 2004, at age ninety-five, *The Wall Street Journal* credited him as the main reason for Columbus' treasure: a "collection of contemporary buildings unrivaled by that of any other American city except New York, Chicago, and Los Angeles."

What Miller did in 1957 was make an offer through the Cummins Foundation to pay the architectural fees for the design of new school buildings. Later, the offer was extended for all public buildings. Since then, the Cummins Foundation has spent around $20 million on more than fifty community projects. Other architectural gems also have been built without benefit of the foundation funds.

A few years ago, when a bridge was erected at the downtown Columbus entrance on Second Street, city leaders demanded a signature structure to fit with the city's reputation as "Athens of the Prairie." The cable-stayed bridge, with four tall red pylons, is lighted at night and frames the 1874 county courthouse and its tower. Designed by J. Muller International and completed in 1999, the Second Street Bridge is the first of its kind in North America. The bridge is fully suspended, and the forty cables that support the structure are in the shape of a fan.

Within a few blocks of the bridge entrance are some of the town's most important contemporary works, including Lincoln Elementary School (Gunnar Birkerts), Cleo Rogers Memorial Library (I. M. Pei), Irwin Union Bank and Trust Co. (Eero Saarinen, son of Eliel Saarinen), Republic newspaper (Myron Goldsmith), Columbus City Hall (Skidmore, Owings & Merrill), Fire Station No. 1 (James K. Paris and Nolan Bingham), Columbus Post Office (Roche Dinkeloo), and North Christian Church (Eero Saarinen).

For Irwin Union Bank, Eero Saarinen designed a new kind of building for a new kind of bank. Projecting a welcoming façade, the bank emphasizes financial services and consumer loans. Instead of the typically imposing bank in heavy stone with classical columns, Union Bank is a low-slung bank encased in glass to emphasize its metaphorical transparency. Rather than having teller cages and barriers, the interior of the human-scaled bank offers a suspended stairway in the center of an open-plan office. The grounds are landscaped like a park.

In the heart of downtown on Second Street, the Bartholomew County Jail is an eye-catcher. Designed by Don M. Hiska & Associates and erected in 1990, the brick-and-limestone jail has no bars on its windows and features a dome on top that allows sunlight to stream inside. The oval-shaped jail is the most dramatic element of the design and is the first of its kind.

The last building designed by Eero Saarinen, who also designed the St. Louis Arch, before his untimely death was the beautiful North Christian Church in Columbus. Eero Saarinen died September 1, 1961, while undergoing surgery for a brain tumor at the age of fifty-one.

Completed in 1964, North Christian Church is a six-sided building that blends with the landscaped earth mound surrounding it. A slender 192-foot spire topped with a gold leaf cross provides a beautiful sky piece. The sanctuary is the center of the church, and the communion table is the center of the sanctuary. Twelve pedestal tables are symbolic of the twelve apostles; a higher pedestal is the Christ table, holding the elements for communion—a silver chalice and a loaf of bread. Worshippers sit facing one another, surrounding the communion table. No one person is farther than forty-eight feet from the pulpit.

Planning for the building, Eero Saarinen wrote to the congregation that his goal "as an architect when I face St. Peter, I am able to say that out of the buildings I did during my lifetime, one of the best was this little church, because it has in it a real spirit that speaks forth to all Christians as a witness to their faith."

THE MILAN
MIRACLE

1954

The score was tied, 30–30. Seconds remained. Bobby Plump crouched, pumped, his right arm thrust. The ball arced through the air amid a roar of screaming and crying fans. He scored.

And tiny Milan High School, one of the state's smallest, made history as the 1954 Indiana state basketball champions. The small-town high school with an entire student body of 161 toppled the powerhouse defending champ, Muncie Central High School, with its enrollment of 2,200.

More than half a century later, that ultimate David versus Goliath story—inspiring the movie *Hoosiers*—is still the heartbeat of Hoosier hysteria. Youngsters tossing hoops in barnyards and make-shift basketball courts are reared by it. It has put the ordinary town near the meandering Ohio River on the map and changed the lives of that amazing team forever.

"If I missed that shot, I wouldn't be talking to you now," Plump says. "It had a very positive influence on every player and anybody associated with that team. It put us in the public eye. There's hardly a day goes by but that I am not reminded of it."

Of the twelve Milan Miracle Men, all but two went on to college; several became coaches. Most still live in Indiana, but none live in Milan. All return often. After graduating from Butler University, Plump played three years for Phillips 66 of the National Industrial Basketball League. Then he began a nearly forty-year career in the life insurance and financial consulting industry. After retiring, Plump opened an Indianapolis restaurant called Plump's Last Shot.

Sports Illustrated named the Milan team one of the top twenty teams of the century. Indiana sports writers chose it as the No. 1 sports story in all of Indiana history. But the heart-stopping last-second win that put a quiet rural town at the top may never come again.

Back then, no attendance classifications separated the largest schools from the smallest in the state tournament. In a state where basketball is king, all competed as equals. In 1997 Indiana ditched its one-classification basketball tournament and divided the schools into four classes.

But, back in 1954, basketball boosters turned their eyes to the Mighty Men of Milan as the team beat its way to the finals. Among their victims was Oscar Robertson's high school team, Crispus Attucks High School in Indianapolis. The "Big O" later went on to be regarded as one of the greatest players in NBA history and was inducted into the National Basketball Association Hall of Fame.

Still, Milan romped past Oscar Robertson and Crispus Attucks. The Milan Indians cruised through the state tournament relatively easily until the final game against the Muncie Central Bearcats. Milan head coach Marvin Wood was just twenty-six years old, and he knew that his players might be intimidated by playing in Indy's enormous Hinkle Fieldhouse where championships were won or lost.

So, just as recounted in the film, Woods measured the height of the basketball goal in Hinkle when his team went to practice to show them that the net was the same height in the huge basketball temple as it was in their tiny Milan gym.

For the final game, Hinkle was packed to the rafters with an estimated 15,000 people. Consider that the whole population of Milan was only 1,150. Among the awestruck fans was player Gene White's mother. She had to sell her chickens early that year so she could go to the championship game.

The fourth quarter of the game is said to be the most famous eight minutes of schoolboy basketball in history. Muncie was ahead. Then Milan. Then Muncie. Then a tie. Plump had the ball with just eighteen seconds remaining. The crowd was on its feet screaming as Plump dribbled the ball down court. Plump glanced at the clock. Six seconds left. Time to make his move. Faking left, then right, Plump edged up to the free throw line, jumped, and shot. Fans who saw it said the large orange orb seemed to arch up and drop in slow motion.

The ball whooshed through the net with three seconds remaining. Milan was the new state champ. Pandemonium erupted. Mobbed by well-wishers and media, Plump and the players needed almost two hours to get back to the locker room. Just as he had promised, Indianapolis motorcycle policeman Pat Stark closed off Monument Circle and escorted the newly crowned boys' champions in a celebratory drive back to their Pennsylvania Hotel rooms around Indiana's best-known landmark.

The next morning, the squad did what it usually did at home. Since it was Sunday, they went to church. Afterward, they ate at the Apex Grill and headed back to Milan in three courtesy Cadillacs, with Pat Stark as an escort again. In those days, there was no fast Interstate 74 linking Indianapolis and Cincinnati. The new champs traveled south on US 421, with the blaring siren of Stark's motorcycle leading the way. The parade quickly began to build. Police cars and fire engines joined in, their sirens wailing in celebration. It took the Indians thirty-five minutes to travel the eighteen miles between Batesville and Sunman where the high school band turned out to greet them.

As the caravan got closer to Milan, the team began to see hastily erected congratulatory signs. Thousands of cars were now lined bumper to bumper for at least thirteen miles along cornfields to Milan. Both sides of the road were crowded with jubilant people waiting for their champs.

Coach Wood's car stopped as the caravan entered Milan. Players Ray Craft and Ken Wendelman got out and rode the rest of the way on the Cadillac hood, holding the state championship trophy between them to share with the crowd. Near the school, even more people were waiting. Estimates placed the huge turnout at about forty thousand people—almost forty times the population of Milan.

Making their way to the flatbed truck stage in front of the school, each player took a turn at the microphone thanking their parents, their coaches, and their community for their support. Said Coach Wood, "Boys like these make my life a dream."

The coach's wife, Mary Lou Wood, added her compliment that "it's nice to be important, but it's more important to be nice."

And still it wasn't over.

There was dinner at the Milan Country Club, then an evening bonfire at Milan High School that burned late into the night. There are those who say the town is still celebrating. A water tower painted with STATE CHAMPS 1954 stands near the railroad tracks. The gold championship trophy sits in a glass case outside the gym in a new school. The old gym was torn down long ago. Nearby is a vintage scoreboard with the final score permanently posted on it: 32–30.

It may never come again to a small Indiana town, but the Milan Miracle is the stuff from which dreams are made, the passion that drives young Hoosiers, and the rallying cry for every small school in the state.

AIDS HITS THE HEARTLAND

1984

Born in Indiana with hemophilia on December 6, 1971, Ryan White was given blood transfusions to deal with his blood coagulation disorder. Even a minor injury could cause severe bleeding for Ryan, so the Kokomo youngster learned early on to deal with his disease and was healthy for most of his childhood.

When he was thirteen, however, Ryan became extremely ill with pneumonia. In December 1984, the teenager was faced with a new diagnosis that would change his life and alter a nation's perceptions. The events that happened in Indiana would shine a spotlight on a worldwide problem.

During a partial lung removal surgery, Ryan was diagnosed with Acquired Immune Deficiency Syndrome, or AIDS. The scientific community knew little of the disease at the time. When Ryan was diagnosed with AIDS, children with the disease were rare. In the public's eye, the only people who had AIDS were gay men. Suddenly, an "innocent" boy, the kid next door, had the frightening disease and the inhumane stigma that went with it.

But Ryan showed the public that everyone is innocent, that no one deserves to have such a devastating illness, and that people with AIDS should be helped and loved, not shunned and tormented.

The 1984 diagnosis was considered a death sentence. Ryan was told that he had no more than six months to live.

Talking it over with his mother, Jeanne White, Ryan decided that he would like to live as normal a life as possible in the time he had left. He wanted to go to school, be with his friends, and do what other normal teens did. However, Ryan's school and community refused to grant the dying boy's wish.

Instead, the local school superintendent barred Ryan from attending school. Teachers and parents were afraid that other children could be contaminated by him. At the time, AIDS and the virus that caused it (HIV) were not understood. Ignorance and fear were widespread. Some thought AIDS could be caught by breathing the same air as a person infected with the disease or that merely touching someone with AIDS could pass it to a healthy person.

Ryan and his family fought the school board's decision. For months, Ryan attended school by telephone as his case passed through the administrative appeals process. When the state ruled that Ryan should be allowed to return to school, that still wasn't the end of his ordeal. A group of parents then sued to keep Ryan out of school. Ultimately, the courts ruled again in Ryan's favor, and he was allowed to return to school.

By then, however, the damage had been done. Ryan was taunted and heard hateful "Ryan White jokes." His school locker was vandalized, his folders were scrawled with the word "fag" and other obscenities. Lies were spread about him and the disease.

To ease the unfounded concerns, Ryan volunteered to use a separate restroom and drinking fountain from other students. He wouldn't attend gym. His eating utensils and tray would be disposable. But it didn't make any difference.

Even though the public knew by then that AIDS was not spread through casual contact, the parents of twenty students started their own school rather than have their children be around Ryan. Even at church, people would shun Ryan. They would refuse to shake his hand, or get up and move if he sat next to them. When Ryan was allowed to return to school for one day in February of 1986, 151 of the school's 360 students stayed home.

Ryan and his family were threatened. When a bullet was fired through the Whites' living room window, the family decided to move to Cicero, Indiana, at the end of the 1986–87 school year.

At the same time, Ryan's struggle was attracting national notice. Suddenly, the teen and his Kokomo hometown were in the news. Letters from strangers poured into the White home, supporting Ryan in his right to attend school. Offering their support and friendship were politicians, top athletes, entertainers, and movie stars, including Elton John, Michael Jackson, Greg Louganis, Charlie Sheen, Alyssa Milano, John Mellencamp, President Ronald Reagan and First Lady Nancy Reagan, coach Bob Knight, and many more. Ryan appeared on numerous television programs, as well as the covers of the *Saturday Evening Post* and *People* magazines.

People sat up and took notice when famous folks hugged Ryan, ate with him, shook his hand, and—in the case of his teen crush, actress Alyssa Milano—kissed him. If they weren't afraid of Ryan, why should anyone else be?

In 1989 a movie about his life, *The Ryan White Story*, was filmed, starring Lukas Haas as Ryan, Judith Light as Jeanne White, Sarah Jessica Parker as a nurse, and George C. Scott as Ryan's attorney.

Ryan made a cameo appearance, playing a boy who has AIDS and is friends with the lead character.

Because of Ryan's numerous interviews and the movie, the soft-spoken, gentle teen suddenly put a human face on the disastrous disease of AIDS. Ryan didn't respond to critics with anger or hatred. He promoted the idea of education and legislation to help AIDS sufferers and dispel the lies about the disease.

At his new home and at Hamilton Heights High School in Cicero, Ryan was greeted with friendship. Instead of giving in to fear, the students had educated themselves about AIDS, and Ryan was finally able to be a teen again. He learned to drive, went to school dances and games, and made the honor roll.

"Hamilton Heights High School is proof that AIDS education in schools works," Ryan testified before the National Commission on AIDS on March 3, 1988. "I'm a normal, happy teenager again."

Ryan was looking forward to his high school graduation, senior prom, and entering Indiana University when he developed a respiratory infection. He was admitted to Riley Hospital for Children in Indianapolis on March 29, 1990. His condition deteriorated rapidly and he was sedated and placed on a ventilator. Well wishes from around the world poured into the hospital.

With his mother, his sister Andrea, his grandparents, his uncle, and his friend Elton John at his bedside, Ryan died on Palm Sunday, April 8, 1990. The teen who had been given only six months to live had defied his prognosis and lived six years. He had opened the hearts and minds of people around the world.

A standing-room-only funeral for Ryan was held on April 11 at the Second Presbyterian Church in Indianapolis with Elton John, talk-show host Phil Donahue, and football star Howie Long as pallbearers. Also attending were Michael Jackson and First Lady Barbara Bush. Ryan was buried in Cicero, near his mother's home.

Since then, Ryan's legacy has continued to grow. Wanting to memorialize the courageous young man, Ryan's friend Jill Stewart started a fund-raising drive at Indiana University. In 1991 IU held its first Dance Marathon. The thirty-six-hour event raised $11,000. The annual event has now raised over $7 million for the children at Riley Hospital. Run entirely by student volunteers, the fund-raiser culminates in the thirty-six-hour marathon every fall. During the marathon weekend, 850 dancers choose to remain awake and standing for thirty-six hours in honor of those children who are unable to do so.

The money also has helped found the Ryan White Infectious Disease Clinic at Riley Hospital for Children where the nation's sickest children are treated. Dr. Martin Kleiman, Ryan's personal physician and good friend, became the Ryan White Professor of AIDS Medicine at Indiana University School of Medicine in Indianapolis.

Inspired by his friendship with Ryan, Elton John created the Elton John AIDS Foundation in 1991. The foundation has raised over $150 million and leveraged an additional $315 million to support HIV/AIDS prevention and programs in fifty-five counties around the world.

Ryan's mother, Jeanne White-Ginder, continues giving speeches and working to help those with HIV/AIDS. She presented the 2010 Ryan White Distinguished Leadership Award to former Surgeon General C. Everett Koop. Established by the Rural Center for AIDS/STD Prevention and HPER at Indiana University, the award was given to Koop for his strong leadership role when the AIDS epidemic was first being recognized. Among other things, Koop spearheaded the unprecedented initiative in the midst of early AIDS hysteria to mail a pamphlet identifying facts and myths about AIDS to 107 million American households.

In 1990, just a few months after Ryan's death, Congress enacted the Ryan White CARE Act, which funds primary health care and support services for people living with HIV/AIDS who lack health insurance and financial resources for their care.

In approving the bill, Senator Edward Kennedy told the Senate: "One thing that was extraordinary, and there are many things about this remarkable young man, was after he received that tainted blood transfusion, to the moment he drew his last breath here on Earth, he never condemned anyone. He was not looking for the scapegoats . . . What he was doing was reaching out in the true spirit of the American character to recognize that there were people who were suffering."

COLTS MOVE TO INDIANAPOLIS

1984

On a dark snowy night in March 1984, the city of Baltimore slept while Mayflower moving vans loaded up and pulled out from suburban Owings Mills. As the snowstorm raged, the big yellow vans headed in all different directions in order to camouflage what was going on. It is said that van drivers didn't even know where they were going or why.

When Baltimore residents awoke the next morning, they were stunned. Their beloved Baltimore Colts football team had left town in the dead of night. Fifteen Mayflower vans had driven about six hundred miles west to the Colts' new home—Indianapolis.

On that red-letter day of March 28, 1984, professional football came to Indy. Since then, the basketball-crazy city has embraced the Indianapolis Colts and will be hosting the 2012 Super Bowl. Colts quarterback Peyton Manning and former coach Tony Dungy are local heroes, not only for their sports expertise but also for their excellent sportsmanship and efforts to help the community and young people in particular.

Peyton Manning Children's Hospital at St. Vincent specializes in treating children with complex, chronic, or congenital conditions. Opened in 2003, the facility was thoughtfully designed for children in a whimsical space that is kid-size and child friendly.

So what caused Baltimore's home team to abandon its fans and end the thirty-year era of the Baltimore Colts?

Ultimately, it was a stadium squabble and dissatisfaction with Baltimore city officials that prompted Colts owner, Robert Irsay, to start looking around for a new home. A self-made millionaire, Irsay had acquired the Colts on July 26, 1972. He got the team by trading his recently purchased Los Angeles Rams to Carroll Rosenbloom for the Colts.

Led by quarterback Johnny Unitas, halfback Lenny Moore, and defensive linemen Art Donovan and Gino Marchetti, the Colts were the top team in the National Football League in the late 1950s. Baltimore fans adored their Colts, and the feeling seemed mutual. Colts players lived among their fans and weren't shy about proclaiming their pride in their hometown. The Baltimore Colts won two World Champions and the 1971 Super Bowl.

Then Robert Irsay took over in 1972. By 1984, Irsay was lobbying the city of Baltimore to improve Memorial Stadium where the Colts played. Irsay claimed he had been promised a new stadium. Baltimore officials denied any such promise was made. Negotiations soured, tempers flared, and Irsay started looking around for a new home for his team. Indianapolis just happened to have a great new stadium, the Hoosier Dome, built in 1983 at a cost of $77.5 million.

Not wanting to lose the Colts, the Maryland state legislature passed a law on March 28, 1984, allowing the city of Baltimore to seize the Colts from Irsay. But it was too late. Irsay accepted a deal offered by the city of Indianapolis and hastily left town shortly after midnight, knowing that the city of Baltimore was about to seize his team at daybreak.

Paving the way to bring the Colts to Hoosier country, Indy Mayor William Hudnut called his friend and neighbor, John Smith—who was also chief executive officer for Mayflower Transit Company headquartered in Indianapolis—and moving vans were on their way. Irsay loaded up his Colts and stole away in the middle of the night. That secretive move is often referred to as "the midnight ride of the Colts."

Baltimore's bid to keep its team slowly proceeded to the federal court. On December 10, 1985, U.S. District Court Judge Walter E. Black Jr. ruled that the team had moved beyond Baltimore's legal reach when the city acted with its eminent domain suit.

Fans in Indianapolis greeted the Mayflower trucks with cheers. In just the first two weeks of ticket sales, the Colts sold 143,000 season tickets. Playing their first game at the Hoosier Dome on September 2, the Colts lost to the New York Jets 23–14. The year ended with a disappointing 4-12 record.

The Colts had other dismal seasons, interspersed with a few hopeful years. The team made the playoffs in 1987, 1995, and 1996. Although their home turf remained the same, the Hoosier Dome name was changed to the RCA Dome in 1994 when RCA paid $10 million for ten-year naming rights. In 1995 the Colts missed winning the AFC Championship game—and a trip to the Super Bowl—when a last-second pass was dropped in the end zone. Robert Irsay died in 1997 and his son Jim Irsay took over the Colts.

When quarterback Peyton Manning arrived in 1998, the Colts became one of the league's most dominant teams. The Indianapolis Colts hosted their first AFC Conference Championship Game in the RCA Dome on January 21, 2007. Before a sellout crowd, the Colts staged the biggest conference championship comeback in history to defeat the New England Patriots, 38–34, and earn their first trip to the Super Bowl since moving to Indiana in 1984. The Colts went on to defeat the Chicago Bears, 29–17, to win the Super Bowl in Miami, Florida. Rain fell throughout the game for the first time in Super Bowl history.

On August 14, 2008, the Colts moved into a brand-new home, the $719 million Lucas Oil Stadium, where football games can be played indoors or outdoors using a retractable roof. The state-of-the-art, 63,000-seat stadium has an infill playing surface, seven locker rooms, exhibit space, meeting rooms, dual two-level club lounges, 137 suites, retractable sideline seating, spacious concourses, and much more. Lucas Oil Stadium is now the permanent home of the Colts and site of the 2012 Super Bowl. The old RCA Dome was demolished on December 20, 2008.

After seven years leading the Colts, Coach Tony Dungy retired in January 2009. Associate head coach Jim Caldwell took over, leading the Colts to a 2010 trip to the Super Bowl, where they lost to the New Orleans Saints, 31–17. Peyton Manning was born in the city of New Orleans, where his father, Archie Manning, was a Saints quarterback.

Although they lost the 2010 title, the Colts compiled a mighty impressive list:

They broke the NFL record for consecutive regular season wins: 23.

They set the league mark for wins in a decade: 115.

They extended their NFL mark of consecutive twelve-win seasons to seven.

They completed seven fourth-quarter comebacks, a league record.

Manning won his fourth MVP award, breaking a tie with Brett Favre for the most ever.

And, as Colts players and fans say, there is always next year.

TIBET AND THE DALAI LAMA COME TO INDIANA

2010

The droning song of a Tibetan violin drifts over the grassy grounds. Incense wafts on the afternoon air. Tibetan dancers move lightly in ritualized harmony. A mandala sand painting created by Buddhist monks gleams in a rainbow of colors and sacred designs.

On a lovely May afternoon in 2010, the Dalai Lama arrives, greeted by hundreds of followers, dignitaries, and media. It is his sixth visit to Bloomington. An unlikely scene? Many think so.

After all, how did a small Hoosier city nestled between rolling hills and cornfields become a regular destination for the fourteenth Dalai Lama, the spiritual and political leader of Tibetans? And how did the place so removed from Tibet become home to the only Tibetan Mongolian Buddhist Cultural Center in the United States?

The answer is simple, although a bit unusual. The Dalai Lama's older brother, Thubten Jigme Norbu, was a professor at Indiana University and lived in Bloomington until his death at age eighty-seven in September 2008. Norbu died at the Chamtse Ling Temple at the Tibetan Mongolian Buddhist Cultural Center where he lived.

Born in 1922 in a small mountain village in Tibet, Norbu was identified at age three as the reincarnation of an important Buddhist lama, Tagtser Rinpoche. As such, he was taken from his home and given the proper education for a high lama. At age twenty-seven, he was appointed abbot of the prestigious Kumbum Monastery in the eastern region of Tibet known as Amdo.

When Red China invaded Tibet in 1950, Norbu was one of the first high-profile Tibetans to go into exile and the first Tibetan to settle in the United States. After he fled Tibet in 1950, he worked to inform the world about the situation in Tibet and gather support for his occupied country.

Herman B Wells, president of Indiana University, heard Norbu speak about Tibet and invited him to teach at the university in Bloomington. That was in 1965. Norbu founded the Tibetan Cultural Center—later renamed the Tibetan Mongolian Buddhist Cultural Center—in 1979. He retired from IU in 1987.

In the meantime, Norbu's younger brother had been proclaimed the fourteenth Dalai Lama. Following the invasion of Tibet by China, Chinese operatives tried to persuade Norbu to work with them and help get rid of the Dalai Lama. The Tibetan people were devoted to the Dalai Lama and China knew it would have a strong ally if Norbu would turn against his brother.

In the Martin Scorsese movie *Kundun*, the character Norbu warns the Dalai Lama that he must escape Tibet because it is too dangerous for him to remain in the Chinese Communist stronghold. Norbu tells his brother that he can work more effectively against the Chinese if he is alive and outside Tibet.

Based on the principles of peace, wisdom, justice, and compassion, the Tibetan Mongolian Buddhist Cultural Center was established in Bloomington on 108 wooded acres on Snoddy Road. The land was a gift from Tom and Kathy Canada. The center's mission is to educate the public about the history, culture, and future of Tibet. It also supports Tibetans both in Tibet and in exile and preserves and shares Tibetan culture, religion, and language. It supports interfaith cooperation and dialogue among all people.

"The temple is open to people of all faiths," said the Venerable Arjia Rinpoche, director of the center. "That was very important to us."

The Dalai Lama has visited the center six times. In 1987, he came to consecrate the Jangclub Chorten, a traditional Buddhist reliquary structure. It stands as a monument to world peace and a memorial to the estimated 1.2 million Tibetans who have perished in the struggle to maintain Tibet's independence. He returned in 1996 to lay the cornerstone of the Kumbum Chamtse Ling, an interdenominational, international temple whose name translates as "Field of Love and Compassion."

In 1999 the Dalai Lama was at the center for fourteen days to consecrate the Kalachakra Stupa and give teachings. He returned in September 2003 with former boxer and peace advocate Muhammad Ali to consecrate the Kumbum Chamtse Ling Temple. In 2007 he visited to change the center's name to the Tibetan Mongolian Buddhist Cultural Center to reflect its broader mission to serve the Mongolian culture. During his 2010 visit, the Dalai Lama gave several teachings on love, peace, and compassion and his first-ever formal press conference.

"I am just a simple Buddhist monk, no more, no less," the Nobel Peace Prize laureate winner often says.

Visiting for the first time since his older brother's death, the Dalai Lama paid tribute to Norbu. "My late brother's spirit still very much lives here, so I am very happy," he said, adding that the center will be his brother's legacy. "The center should be a learning center, not just a place for worship."

Open to the public, the center is the only place in the United States where people can see traditional Tibetan Chortens, yak butter sculptures, and a permanent sand mandala, as well as learn about Tibetan culture through teachings and special events.

It may also be the only place in America where a high Buddhist lama was cremated in a traditional Tibetan ceremony.

After Norbu died in 2008, special permission had to be gained from local and state officials to build a brick and clay cremation structure behind the center's temple. On the day of the funeral, five days after his death, Norbu's body was arranged sitting on a bed in a lotus position. He was dressed in elaborate garments and headgear. Visitors were given colored katas or prayer scarves to present to Norbu's sons, who placed them on their father's bed. Tibetan monks from across the country chanted and sang prayers during the ritual. The Dalai Lama didn't make it for the funeral. The Dalai Lama lives in India where he has established the Tibetan Government-in-Exile.

Norbu's three sons—Jigme, Lhundrup, and Kunga—along with volunteers carried Norbu's body to the crematorium structure, where he was placed inside. Constructed of unfired brick and covered with clay, the cremation structure was then filled with cedar wood and soaked with pure essential oils. The vessel was closed with brick and clay, leaving ventilation openings at the bottom, top, and sides. The small crematorium was lighted and burned for more than two hours.

For the next forty-nine days, special prayers were said on each seventh day to help Norbu in his rebirth. The reincarnated lama would be born within those forty-nine days, choosing where and when he would be reborn. It would be his twenty-fourth rebirth.

As early as 2011, the Dalai Lama will lead a search party to find the reincarnated lama Tagtser Rinpoche. Buddhist monks seeking reincarnated souls usually look for clues the person might have left behind in the previous life. The investigation is "very mysterious," the Dalai Lama acknowledged, and would take some meditation.

"My elder brother is a very sincere person, a very dedicated person. We respect him," the Dalai Lama said on his Bloomington visit. "However, when his death took, he was already very old. So that is the normal way to go."

As for what Buddhism can offer Western societies, the Dalai Lama said that Buddhism as a religion "belongs to the East" and is not needed in the West with its Judeo-Christian traditions. However, Buddhism concepts about achieving inner peace can be useful to all people, he said.

"All major religions traditionally all have the same potential to bring inner peace through the practice of love, compassion, forgiveness, tolerance, contentment," the Dalai Lama said. "The real source of happiness is within ourselves."

INDIANA FACTS AND TRIVIA

- The Hoosier city of Columbus is ranked sixth in the nation for architectural innovation and design by the American Institute of Architects on a list that includes the much larger cities of Chicago, New York, Boston, San Francisco, and Washington, D.C.

- Despite its Cajun-sounding name, Boudreaux's Butt Paste is manufactured in Columbus at Blairex Laboratories, Inc. The popular ointment with the unusual name is known for its ability to wipe out diaper rash and other skin irritations.

- The Little 500 at Indiana University in Bloomington is the nation's largest collegiate bicycling event. Started in 1951, the relay race features four-member student teams pedaling around a quarter-mile cinder track.

- The nickname of the sports teams for Vincennes Lincoln High School is the "Alices." The school picked that name in honor of local author Maurice Thompson, who wrote the 1900 book *Alice of Old Vincennes*, set during the American Revolution.

- Although Military Park in Indianapolis was a Civil War encampment, the fourteen-acre green space drew its name not from its past but from its shape—like a military badge.

- Deep below the earth in southern Indiana is a sea of limestone that is one of the richest deposits of top-quality limestone found anywhere on Earth. New York City's Empire State Building and Rockefeller Center; the Pentagon, the

U.S. Treasury, and a dozen other government buildings in Washington, D.C.; and fourteen state capitols around the nation are built from this sturdy, beautiful Indiana limestone.

- From 1886 to 1919, industrialist Andrew Carnegie built 1,679 public libraries across the United States. Indiana benefited the most with 164 libraries.

- More than one hundred species of trees are native to Indiana. Before the pioneers' arrival more than 80 percent of Indiana was covered with forest. Now only 17 percent of the state is considered forested.

- True to its motto, "Crossroads of America," Indiana has more miles of interstate highway per square mile than any other state, and more major highways intersect in Indiana than in any other state.

- The only animal named for the state, the endangered Indiana bat, was discovered in 1928 in Wyandotte Cave near Leavenworth.

- Indianapolis Motor Speedway earned the nickname "The Brickyard" because it was once paved with 3.2 million bricks. Only the start/finish line, known as the "yard of bricks," is still exposed today.

- Motorists used gas lamps, candles, and oil lamps for night driving before Carl G. Fisher manufactured the first practical sealed-beam gas headlight, Prest-O-Lite, in 1904 in Indianapolis. Fisher was born January 12, 1874, in Greensburg, Indiana.

- When Captain Charles Gerard Conn suffered a bruised lip, he didn't hang up his cornet. Instead, the Elkhart man invented a soft rubber mouthpiece for his musical instrument. When other people wanted the same soft mouthpiece, Conn began making the items in a home workshop. In 1875 Conn began manufacturing brass cornets, and his business became the first wind instrument factory in the nation.

- Named after a Native American word whose meaning has been lost, Nappanee may be the only town in the world that uses all of its letters twice.

- Indianapolis is called "The Circle City," a little boy said, because cars at the Indy 500 drive in circles for hours. A cute story, but the nickname came from Alexander Ralston's nineteenth-century street layout based on concentric circles. At the very center is Monument Circle with the 284-foot-tall Soldiers and Sailors Monument in the middle.

- Richard Gatling, an Indianapolis physician, invented the world's first rapid-firing machine gun in 1862. An early model fired two hundred shots a minute. By 1898, the Gatling gun could fire three thousand rounds a minute. Dr. Gatling envisioned his gun as a weapon so terrible that it would end war forever.

- The town of Reo in Spencer County got its name from the acronym of three nearby cities: Rockport and Evansville in Indiana and Owensboro in Kentucky.

- The tradition for winners of the Indianapolis 500 to drink milk in Victory Lane began in 1936 when Indy winner Louis Meyer refreshed himself with cold buttermilk.

- Indianapolis and Oklahoma City are the only state capitals with the name of the state in the name of the city.

- Ninety percent of the world's popcorn is grown in Indiana.

- A statue of a popular 1940s comic book hero, boxing champ Joe Palooka, stands near city hall in Oolitic. The statue was carved from Bedford limestone to celebrate the centennial of the region's limestone industry and was dedicated in 1948.

- In 1921 Elmer Cline of Taggart Baking Co. in Indianapolis needed a name for the company's new 1.5-pound loaf of bread. When he saw a balloon race and felt a sense of wonder at the colorful balloons floating through the air, he was struck with the inspired name of Wonder Bread.

- Hulman and Co. of Terre Haute (population 59,614), makers of Clabber Girl Baking Powder, created a product that was a great boon to cooks. Before the 1879 introduction of manufactured leaveners, bakers mixed sour (or clabbered) milk with a form of baking soda. The mixture would release carbon dioxide into the dough, causing it to rise. Manufactured baking powder produced a more consistent and reliable result.

- Blind and sensitive to the jerky movements of automobiles, automotive pioneer Ralph Teetor of Hagerstown invented cruise control. Patenting his device in 1945, Teetor was said to be inspired by the stop-and-go, choppy driving of his attorney.

- Harmless freshwater jellyfish have found a home at Patoka Lake, near Birdseye. About the size of a quarter, the healthy jellyfish are said to be an indicator that the 8,800-acre reservoir has a pure and clean ecosystem.

- In the late 1800s, J.S. McQuinn founded Hoosier Manufacturing Co. in Albany to build the freestanding kitchen cabinet he invented to include storage and work space. The innovative cabinet style is still called a "Hoosier" and has become a collector's prize.

- Born on Valentine's Day 1913, in Brazil, Indiana, James "Jimmy" Hoffa grew up to become a controversial labor leader. His disappearance on July 30, 1975, remains an unsolved mystery, despite one of the largest FBI manhunts in history. Ironically, Hoffa's middle name was Riddle.

- Only two places in the world boast the unusual paper coal: central Russia and Parke County. A rare relic of the Coal Age, paper coal is so called because it resembles scorched paper. The fragments of seed ferns in Indiana's paper coal have been extinct for more than two hundred million years.

- Indiana was the first state in the country to commercially produce wine. The industry began in Vevay in 1802.

- Opened in 1888, Union Station in Indianapolis was the nation's first union railway depot. A young Thomas Edison worked there as a Western Union telegraph operator.

- In 1923 Carmel installed what is believed to be the first electric traffic light in the United States. Because it had only red and green lights, motorists were unable to judge when the signal would change and were constantly running the red light.

BIBLIOGRAPHY

Cave Saves Squire Boone's Life—1790

Squire Boone Caverns, personal visit and observations by the author.

Battle of Tippecanoe—1811

Battle Ground, personal visit and observations by the author.

Grouseland in Vincennes, personal visit and observations by the author.

Immell, Myra H. and William H., *The Importance of Tecumseh.* San Diego, California: Lucent Books, 1997.

Shorto, Russell, *Tecumseh and the Dream of an American Indian Nation.* Englewood Cliffs, New Jersey: Silver Burdett Press, 1989.

Stefoff, Rebecca, *Tecumseh and the Shawnee Confederation.* New York, New York: Facts on File, 1998.

New Harmony Settled as a Utopian Community—1814

New Harmony, personal visit and observations by the author.

Abraham Lincoln Moves to Indiana—1816

Colonel William Jones Home, personal visit and observations by the author.

Lincoln Amphitheatre, personal visit and observations by the author.

Lincoln Boyhood National Memorial & Living Historical Farm, personal visit and observations by the author.

Lincoln Pioneer Village and Museum, personal visit and observations by the author.

Lincoln State Park, personal visit and observations by the author.

Spencer County, personal visit and observations by the author.

Levi Coffin and the Underground Railroad—1820s–1840s

Coffin, Levi, *Reminiscences of Levi Coffin,* Cincinnati: Robert Clarke Company, 1898.

Hendrick, George and Willene. *Fleeing for Freedom,* Chicago: Ivan R. Dee, 2004.

Levi Coffin House, personal visit and observations by author.

State Capital Moves to Indianapolis—1824

Corydon, personal visit and observations by the author.

DAR, *Story of Indiana's Constitution Elm.* Corydon, Indiana: General Printing Co., 1974.

Finch, Jackie Sheckler, *Insiders' Guide to Indianapolis.* Guilford, Connecticut: Globe Pequot, 2010.

Indianapolis, personal visit and observations by the author.

The Fall Creek Massacre—1824

Conner Prairie, Indiana, personal visit and observations by the author.

Smith, Oliver Hampton, *Early Indiana Trials and Sketches.* Cincinnati, Ohio: Moore Wilstach, Keys and Co., 1858.

Gold Discovered in Brown County—1830s

Brown County, personal visit and observations by the author.

Trail of Death—1838

Potawatomi Trail of Death Regional Historic Trail 1838, Indiana to
Kansas, personal visit and observations by the author.

South Bend, personal visit and observations by the author.

Winger, Otto, *The Potawatomi Indians.* Elgin, Illinois: Elgin Press,
1939.

Santa Claus Comes to Town—1852

Interview with Pat Koch by the author.

Santa Claus, personal visit and observations by the author.

Santa Claus Museum, personal visit and observations by the author.

Studebakers Start Building Wagons—1852

Smallzried, Kathleen Ann, and James Roberts, *More Than You
Promise.* New York, New York: Harper & Brothers Publishers,
1942.

South Bend, Indiana, personal visit and observations by the author.

John Hunt Morgan's Raid—1863

Corydon and Madison County, personal visit and observations by
the author.

John Hunt Morgan Trail driving brochure.

Explosion Aboard the *Argosy*—1865

Magnet, personal visit, and observations by the author.

BIBLIOGRAPHY

First United States Train Robbery—1866

Seymour, personal visit and observations by the author.

Discovery of Marengo Cave—1883

Marengo Cave, personal visit and observations by the author.

Dan Patch, The Greatest Pacer Horse of Them All—1896

Eugene and Marilyn Glick Indiana History Center in Indianapolis, personal visit and observations by the author.

Oxford, Indiana, personal visit and observations by the author.

The First Indy 500—1911

Finch, Jackie Sheckler, *Insiders' Guide to Indianapolis.* Guilford, Conn.: Globe Pequot Press, 2010.

Indianapolis Motor Speedway, personal visit and observations by the author.

Kramer, Ralph, *Indianapolis Motor Speedway—100 Years of Racing.* Iola, Wisconsin: Krause Publications, 2009.

First Transcontinental Radio Broadcast of a Funeral—1931

Robinson, Ray, *Rockne of Notre Dame.* New York, New York: Oxford University Press, 1999.

South Bend, personal visit and observations by the author.

Stuhldreher, Harry, *Knute Rockne All American.* New York, New York: Grosset & Dunlap, 1931.

John Dillinger Escapes from Jail—1934

Crown Point, personal visit and observations by the author.

Gorn, Elliott J., *Dillinger's Wild Ride*. New York, New York: Oxford University Press, 2009.

Matera, Dary, *John Dillinger*. New York, New York: Carroll & Graf Publishers, 2004.

Haunted Willard Library—1937

Evansville, personal visit and observations by the author.

Willard Library, personal visit and observations by the author.

Columbus Architectural Birth Starts—1942

Columbus, personal visit and observations by the author.

Mote, Patricia M., *Images of America – Columbus*. Charleston, S.C.: Arcadia Publishing, 2005.

The Milan Miracle—1954

Dobrovodsky, Roger, and Honeywell, Ken. *Last of the Small Town Heroes*. Indianapolis, Indiana: Good Morning Publishing Co., Inc., 1997.

Finch, Jackie Sheckler, *Insiders' Guide to Indianapolis*. Guilford, Conn.: Globe Pequot Press, 2010.

Interview with Bobby Plump by the author.

Milan, personal visit and observations by the author.

AIDS Hits the Heartland—1984

Hearing Ryan's mother, Jeanne White-Ginder, give a speech.

The Ryan White Story movie.

www.RyanWhite.com.

BIBLIOGRAPHY

Colts Move to Indianapolis—1984

Baltimore Sun archives.

Indianapolis Hoosier Dome, RCA Dome, and Lucas Oil Stadium, personal visits and observations by the author.

Indianapolis Star archives.

Tibet and the Dalai Lama Come to Indiana—2010

Interview with the Dalai Lama by the author.

Tibetan Mongolian Buddhist Culture Center, personal visit and observations by the author.

Indiana Facts and Trivia

American Profile magazine, Franklin, Tennessee.

Finch, Jackie Sheckler, *Insiders' Guide to Indianapolis.* Guilford, Conn.: Globe Pequot Press, 2010.

INDEX

ABOUT THE AUTHOR

Jackie Sheckler Finch is an award-winning journalist and photographer who has called Indiana her home for more than two decades. A Bloomington resident, she moved from Massachusetts and began working for *The Herald-Times* in 1989, covering city government and other beats. She is now *The Herald-Times* travel writer and is editor of two Indiana magazines—*Adventure Indiana* and *Homes & Lifestyles of South Central Indiana*. She is a freelance writer for such publications as *AAA Home & Away* and *American Profile* and Web sites such as Triporati, Examiner.com, Suite 101, and GirlfriendsThatGolf.com.

She is also the author of ten books, including *Insiders' Guide to Indianapolis, Insiders' Guide to Nashville,* and *Tennessee Off the Beaten Path* (all published by Globe Pequot Press). She was named the Mark Twain Travel Writer of the Year by Midwest Travel Writers a record four times, in 1998, 2001, 2003, and 2006, and is also a member of The Society of American Travel Writers.

Jackie shares her Hoosier home with Pepper, resident guard dog and entertainer. One of her greatest joys is taking to the road to find the fascinating people and places that wait over the hill and around the next bend.